Christof Weiss

SNOW BOARDING EXPERTS

BARRON'S

Christof Weiss

SNOW BOARDING EXPERTS

Freeriding—Race—Freestyle

Text of the original German edition:
SNOWBOARDING EXPERTS
© 1996 BLV Verlagsgesellschaft mbH, Munchen/Germany

Translated from the German by Eric A. Bye, M.A.

All inquiries should be addressed to:
Barron's Educational Series, Inc.
250 Wireless Boulevard
Hauppauge, NY 11788
http://www.barronseduc.com

Library of Congress Catalog Card No. 98-22823

International Standard Book No. 0-7641-0738-0

Library of Congress Cataloging-in-Publication Data
Weiss, Christof.
    [Snowboarding Experts.   English]
    Snowboarding experts / Christof Weiss ; translated
from the German by Eric A. Bye.
        p.   cm.
    Includes bibliographical references (p.).
    ISBN 0-7641-0738-0
    1. Snowboarding.   I. Title.
GV857.S57W4213   1998
796.9—dc21
                                        98-22823
                                        CIP

Printed in Hong Kong
9 8 7 6 5 4 3 2 1

**With cooperation from Martin Freinademetz,
Sigi Prey (Racing), and Reto Lamm (Freestyle)**
Photo credits:
Hermann Bohler: p. 156 top
Department of Nature and Environmental Protection of
the DAV: p. 156, middle, bottom
Katja Delago: p. 79
Stefan Eisend: pp. 10–11, 20 top, 22 bottom, 26, 36, 47, 57,
66 (2), 67 top, 67 middle right, bottom right, 68, 70, 85
left, 89, 99 top, 104, 161
Andrew Hourmont: pp. 22 top, 76–77, 84
Peter Mathis: pp. 2–3, 6 right, 7 right, 74–75, 85 right, 87 (2),
93, 110, 112, 113 bottom, 115 (2), 119 top, left bottom,
121 (2), 122 top and middle, 126, 127, 128, 129 middle,
130, 131, 133 (2), 134, 135 (2), 136, 137, 138, 140 (2), 141,
143, 145, 146 (2), 148, 152, 153, 155 (2), 157 top right, 163
Herman Seidl: pp. 6 left, 7 left and middle (2), 8–9, 14, 19,
23 (6), 24 (2), 25, 27, 39 (2), 41 (2), 44 (2), 45, 49, 50 (2),
51 (2), 53, 55, 58 (2), 60, 62 (4), 63 (6), 64 (2), 65, 81, 91,
92, 95 (4), 99 left bottom, 100 bottom, 102, 103 top, 105
(8), 107 bottom, 113 top, 114 (2) 123 top, 124–25, 129 top
(2) and bottom (2), 132 (2), 144, 157 middle and bottom
Richard Walch: pp. 1, 21, 83 top, 86, 88, 90, 107 top, 119
middle, 154

Christof Weiss earned a degree in sports science in 1965. He has actively followed the development of the new discipline of snowboarding since its inception and has dedicated himself to becoming a snowboarding instructor and extreme freerider. He is a consultant to several snowboard companies as well as to various sports magazines. He has already made a name for himself as a sports author with the volume *Snowboarding Know-how* and with the editing of *Sport Cycling Handbook*, both of which have been issued by BLV Publishing, Inc. In the summer this cycling enthusiast exchanges his snowboard for a mountain bike or a road bike to keep in shape for the next season.

Wojciech Zwierzynski: pp. 17, 20 bottom, 28, 29, 34, 48, 67
left middle and left, 72, 77 top, 78, 80, 82, 83 bottom, 94,
119 lower right, 122 bottom, 123 bottom, 147

Cover photo: Peter Mathis
Back cover photos: Peter Mathis (2), Herman Seidl
Cover design: Sander and Krause Agency
Graphics: Huber Cartography, Daniela Farnhammer
Editorial Office: Karin Steinback
Layout: Steinbicker Studio, Munich
Production: Manfred Sinicki
BLV Publishing, Inc.
Munich, Vienna, Zurich

The Idea

Snowboarding has already experienced incredibly fast development. The roots that have nourished snowboarding and made it what it is today include the abundance of experiences, the fascination with motion, the outlook on life, and the individuality that it offers.

The advanced development this sport has reached is demonstrated in many ways, including level of performance, board technology, and competitions. This development is evident in how close performance results are and in the disciplines' stress profiles.

Systematic and purposeful training has been applied to racing for some time now, and it's beginning to gain a hold in Freestyle. Snowboarding technique is closely linked to progress in performance, which is the gauge for changes in all of snowboarding.

Participating in competitions is now possible at practically any level of mastery. Great popularity and interest in competitive events are reflected in starting fields and in the development of new disciplines such as Boardercross. The continually evolving variety of snowboarding points to the realm of Freeriding, where more and more snowboarders seek the ultimate experience. But parallel to all these trends, people are increasing their needs and expectations from the sport. This applies to the ambitious snowboarding beginner as well as to the top-level performer and to various special interest groups. The nature of the sport is subject to huge pressure in expectations that has turned it into an established and commercialized high-performance sport, and has pushed the original character of snowboarding into the background.

Mutual testing of one's abilities is undoubtedly a unique feature of humans, and it's natural that it should find a solid place in snowboarding. But further development requires new beginnings. This book aims to provide a possible beginning. It seems that the proper time has come for a more comprehensive examination of the discipline and of its athletic components. Several companies that continually supported this book project felt the same way. But the basic idea is not in the isolated presentation of distinct disciplines, but rather in the conscious integration of the original motives of variety of experiences, fascination with motion, outlook on life, and individuality in snowboard training. Only this consciousness can preserve for us in the future the all-important, essential character of snowboarding.

Individual themes will be complemented and clarified with outstanding visuals. Photos elucidate and clarify. They help the motivated beginner as well as the advanced and top-level snowboarder. The book is thus intended to serve as an individual training advisor; it contains lots of background information. Snowboarders can deliberately and consciously shape their athletic development, whether in preparation for competition or merely to improve their skills.

At this point I wish to thank my collaborators Sigi Prey, Martin Freinademetz, and Reto Lamm, as well as the photographers Peter Mathis, Herman Seidl, Stefan Eisend, Wojciech Zwierzynski, Andrew Hourmont, Richard Walch, Katja Delago, Hermann Bohler, and the Nature and Environment Department of the DAV. This book was made possible only through this cooperation. Further support came from Christine Rauter, Dieter Happ, Dieter Krassinig, Fabien Rohrer, Anita Schwaller, Juha Sulkakoski, Hannu Laakkonen, Kiwi Meier, Hermann Bohler, and Jurgen Mitternacht. I'm also grateful to the following companies for their exemplary cooperation: Fire and Ice; Rad Air; Nitro; Burton; Raichle; Arnet; Ortovox; Lowe Alpine; Rohner, Level, Kaindl, and Partners; Toko; Swix; Bordercross Marketing and Consulting, Inc.; Saas Fee Cable Car; Inc., and Kaunertal Glacier Track, Inc.

Christof Weiss

Have fun training
and snowboarding!

C O N T E N T S

Race

The incredibly fast development of snowboarding, its variety, and its fascination with movement are reflected in the realm of racing. Racing has contributed significantly to the appeal of this sport. Racing has lent an important stimulus to the development of equipment and technique and has helped make this sport popular all over the world.

Every winter the International Snowboard Federation (ISF) conducts a World Pro Tour consisting of a number of competitions in Europe, the United States, Argentina, Australia, and Japan.

Aside from this international race series for the best snowboarders in the world, other snowboarding associations put on countless events every year in North America alone. With these competitions all snowboarders who are interested in racing have a chance to get to the starting gate. The growth in starting fields at these events shows the great interest in the entire sport and in racing. The development of the World Pro Tour and the national events have produced many competitors who perform at similar levels. As this compacting increases, so does the pressure to perform, and with it the need to advance to a higher level. This development calls for systematic training.

Suddenly snowboarding—an experience-oriented fun sport with its own outlook—faces a focus on performance. The danger of losing snowboarding's fundamental qualities should not be overlooked. But perhaps the mentality of the snowboarder and the value of the adventure will continue to characterize this performance-oriented sport in the future.

Snowboarding stands for individuality. That is perhaps the only bridge that connects the performance

sport to snowboarding's attitude on life. But present attitudes on general performance lose some of their significance if the performance sport leaves no room for individuality.

Snowboarding has a unique opportunity to take a slightly different route than other sports have taken.

Training makes the fun and variety of experience compatible with the performance sport. The resulting views and experiences open a way to achieve this goal.

The great popularity of racing calls for general availability of the best information on individual training. That is always based on the supreme principle of individuality. The observations and experiences are not conceived just for aspiring snowboarding racers, but are universally applicable to the entire sport of snowboarding.

The first training for racing was based on experience from ski racing. But as time went on specific differences in technical needs and stress profile became evident. From that point on, snowboarding developed its own training methodology. More and more snowboarders are gaining access to race disciplines. They do this for various reasons. Some wish to be successful on national or even on international levels. Others ride the courses purely for fun, wish to improve their technique, or seek challenge, variety, and success.

Independently of personal goals many riders pursue a specific plan. But because of insufficient knowledge, the snowboarder often forgets or doesn't even know the "how-to."

The present starting point should make this training "how-to" accessible and help snowboarders to organize their goals. It provides a guide for planning a training program to help snowboarders reach their goals. This applies to beginners as well as to top-flight snowboarders. The principles are always the same, even though the specifics are different depending on needs and goals.

But before we follow the road to systematic and individual race training, we need some basic information on general training theory.

Today's snowboard races fascinate with their exceptional dynamism of movement

BASICS

Anyone whose standards lead them to pursue specific goals in racing should, in the capacity of athlete or trainer, have a good look at some basics of training theory. An understanding of these basics leads to the better organization of training and avoids training without a plan.

Only with this basic knowledge can one really grasp what follows. In the course of this chapter the connections between theory and training practice will become clear. Readers are invited to find out more by consulting references provided at the end of this book.

Training and Training Theory

The term *training* usually denotes a process that seeks a more or less distinct degree of progress toward attaining goals. In this context, Martin sees in training a process that produces change in the physical, motor, cognitive, and affective realms.

Training theory is a part of sport theory that deals with the athlete in training. Its findings are supported partly by empirical knowledge (e.g., medicine, psychology, and biomechanics) and by generalized subjective experiences of athletes and trainers.

The resulting ground rules for training are useful as guidelines for training practice. But they are not to be taken as invariably or directly applicable; rather, they are subject to individual experiences of athletes and trainers and must be considered in the context of any given situation. Athletic training is seen as a pedagogical and biologic outlet, and is therefore defined as a methodically guided process to bring about change in complex athletic ability (see Fig. I).

Complex Athletic Ability

Complex athletic ability is subject to five factors that come into play simultaneously, and is regarded as a product of one's ability and readiness to perform. Individual factors should always be considered together, and never separately.

Complex athletic ability provides the basis for systematic snowboarding training.

Fig. I: Factors that influence athletic ability; the five areas should not be considered separately, since they interact, according to Zintl.

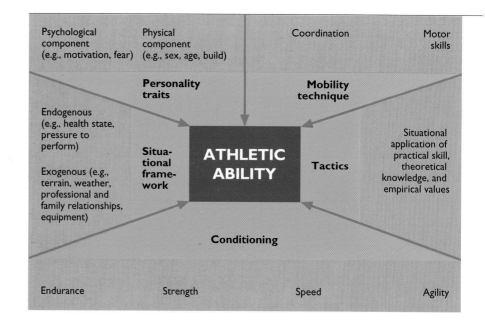

| Psychological component (e.g., motivation, fear) | Physical component (e.g., sex, age, build) | | Coordination | Motor skills |

Personality traits — **Mobility technique**

Endogenous (e.g., health state, pressure to perform)

Situational framework — **ATHLETIC ABILITY** — **Tactics** — Situational application of practical skill, theoretical knowledge, and empirical values

Exogenous (e.g., terrain, weather, professional and family relationships, equipment)

Conditioning

| Endurance | Strength | Speed | Agility |

Conditioning

These abilities relate primarily to the generation of energy and to the makeup of the organ system. The previously mentioned combination of coordination and conditioning abilities figure into a complex examination of these skills. These have energy as well as neural causes. Conditioning is usually divided into endurance, strength, speed, and agility; these are the bases for ability among snowboarders.

Mobility Technique

Mobility technique is one of the basic factors of complex athletic ability in snowboarding. It stems jointly from coordination and from motor skills.

Coordination consists of management and control of movement. Specific categories include abilities to react, connect (spatially), orient, rhythmize (kinesthetically), differentiate, and anticipate (see p. 49).

A special form of these abilities is the combined coordination/conditioning abilities. Agility and the various strength and speed skills fall into this category.

Motor skills are automatic movements and are part of an entire motion. In snowboarding these can be vertical and diagonal movements for weighting and unweighting the board, for controlling the board, or for running gates. In contrast to inherent abilities (talent), skills can be learned and made automatic through practice.

Personality Traits

These characteristics refer to the physical as well as to the psychological makeup of the athlete. Physical conditions include age, sex, and build or body weight.

Psychological abilities include the athlete's affective and cognitive abilities. In competition they become defining factors. As a result, they should be given special consideration in training for snowboard racing.

The factors of motivation, pleasure, ability to concentrate, and fear are significant in regard to athletic skill.

Tactics

Tactics refers broadly to the situational application of practical ability, theoretical knowledge, and experience in order to produce optimal athletic success. Tactics are formed by perception (including sensory), combination, and thought processes. These factors play an important role within a snowboarding competition relative to the numerous qualification runs and should be developed and furthered by a long-term training program.

Situational Framework

The framework can be personal (endogenous) as well as situational (exogenous).

The endogenous framework refers to the athlete's conditioning. It includes state of health, talent, and existing motivation to perform.

The exogenous framework acts on the athlete from the outside, and in training and competition it can become a highly limiting factor. Variation in training is an important contribution to the racer's development. This framework includes terrain, weather, equipment, and even personal relationships.

These frameworks are an important foundation for assessment and analysis of training and competition in snowboarding.

Training Principles

Several areas with great general validity, including training principles, have developed within training theory. They amount to extremely important instructions for the training process. In the following pages only a small part of these fundamentals will be addressed. They relate to instruction and to biology. These principles will be illustrated and clarified with examples taken from snowboard training.

Background of TRAINING PRINCIPLES

	PRINCIPLE
Relating to instruction	Awareness
	Clarity
	Appropriateness
Relating to biology	Effective stress stimulus
	Progressive stress (gradual and rapid)
	Variation in training load
	Optimal structuring of stress and recovery
	Repetition and continuity
	Periodic and cyclic training
	Individuality and age appropriateness
	Increased specialization
	Adjustment of interaction
	Individual training elements

The Awareness Principle

This principle refers to the awareness that athletes have of the immediate and long-range goals of their activity. The responsibility for this is placed on the athletes themselves.

Before snowboarders begin training for competition they should consider

- Why they are starting the training (or a specific type of training)
- Why they are taking on this commitment
- What other things in life may (or must not be) neglected as a result
- If they are prepared to make sacrifices

The Clarity Principle

Clarity is very important for all age groups. In this case it refers to a clear understanding of the training measures the trainer has chosen for the athlete.

An important consideration here is the varied acuity of the athlete's sensory perception (visual, verbal, and motor).

These perception factors play an important role in snowboarding. They must be adapted to different individuals and ages. With

youngsters, for example, a particular snowboarding technique can be demonstrated by the trainer. On the other hand, with adults, verbal clarity is more important. Training instructions and clarifications are more effective when delivered through personal conversation. Needless to say, this does not entail a mere one-sided imparting of information from the trainer to the athlete. The athlete must assume the responsibility for providing the trainer with important information, ideas, and instructions for putting together the training program (see the section on the Awareness Principle).

In every training session the Clarity Principle is of great importance.

The Appropriateness Principle

This fundamental relates to the development of the athlete's abilities. Appropriateness signifies the correct relationship between present performance capacity and the stress requirements that lie at the upper edge of one's ability, but that should not be exceeded.

Stress requirements are keyed to the athlete's overall circumstances. Appropriateness should fall between the athlete's desired level and ability.

Appropriateness of training is often overlooked in snowboarding. At this point we should refer again to the Awareness Principle. For example, if training is conducted in poor visibility, even though technical problems can be detected on the same course in good visibility, the performance doesn't correspond to the stress requirement. This overloading can lead to stagnation and setbacks in performance; it should always be avoided. ▪

The Principle of Effective Stress Stimulus

The biologic rule of stimulus forms the basis of this fundamental principle. It distinguishes between stimuli that are subliminal (below effective threshold), weak, strong, and too strong.

Subliminal stimuli have no effect; weak ones maintain functional level; strong ones improve functional level; and stimuli that are too strong are harmful to functioning. Application of stimuli is therefore dependent upon the following stress components:

Frequency of training (number of training sessions per day or per week)
Extent of stimulus (duration and number of stimuli per training session)
Density of stimuli (temporal relationship between stress and recovery phases)
Intensity of stimuli (strength of individual stimuli)
Duration of stimuli (effective duration of a stimulus or set of stimuli)

According to this principle, the beginning racer should not move too quickly from increasing the number of training sessions per week or per month to the other four loading components. In general a rider's body needs adequate time to get used to the selected stress. With beginners the Principle of Awareness, especially concerning investment of training time (per week, month, or year) also plays a fundamental role. ▪

Principle of Progressively Increasing Stress

A progressively increasing load is usually reached via a change in stress components. That makes sense in the sequence just mentioned. But an increased load can result also from higher coordination demands and from a greater number of races.

Coordination demands become greater as performance improves.
At top levels, they are of crucial importance and are characterized especially by steeper terrain, greater speeds, and more difficult courses. ▪

Principle of Varying Training Load

An unvarying training load leads to monotony and to stagnating returns from training. Improvement can be effected by varying the workout load. In actual training that is accomplished by varying the intensity and amount, plus varying the motion dynamics, the selection of exercises, and the type of breaks.

The number of training runs in a workout must include meaningful variation. So particularly intense workouts should be followed by training sessions of lower intensity that allow for recovery. These variations can also be incorporated into individual training sessions. ▪

Principle of Optimal Stress and Recovery

In this principle we find one of the most important and most frequently overlooked fundamentals of training theory. Riders who disregard it will find it difficult or impossible to reach their goals. It regards stress and recovery practically as a single unit. As a fundamental principle of biology, that phenomenon leads to overcompensation (see Fig. 2), which basically reflects the temporal nature of the recovery process following stress. In the phases of stress and recovery there can be excessive recovery and a subsequent decline back to the starting level.

The next stress in the overcompensation phase should be carried out in accordance with the overcompensation model in order to produce the most favorable structuring of stress and recovery.

In view of the principle explained above, snowboarders should always train to improve their jumping ability and speed, since these factors are so crucial to riding technique. It should be made clear that conditioning (including strength) and coordination (such as action and reaction speed) form the basis of this principle. That's why this fundamental principle is of such significance in all aspects of training for snowboarding. ▬▬

Fig. 2: Overcompensation (OC) according to Zintl (1990)
Phases of Change in Ability:
1 = Declining phase
2 = Recovery phase (compensation)
3 = Overcompensation phase (excessive compensation)
4 = Fluctuation phase (reversion)

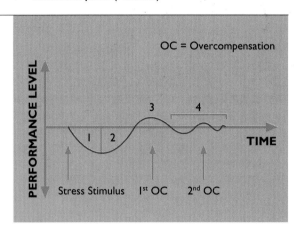

Principle of Repetition and Continuity

For the best adjustment of the body to stress it is important to repeat the stress numerous times. The controlling structures of the central nervous system need a long time—even several months—to adjust.

The level of technical training should provide the developing snowboarder ample time (several weeks) for the best adjustment of coordination. Demands that are increased too quickly will lead in the long run to a setback rather than to improvement. ▬▬

Periodic and Cyclic Principle

Athletes can not remain at peak conditioning all-yearlong. Otherwise they are continually at the upper limit of their ability to withstand stress. On biologic grounds a change in load is therefore important. In the long run (training year[s]), the course of adjustment, which is characterized by different phases, requires a gradation in increasing, stabilizing, and diminishing periods of stress (preparation, competition, and transition periods); in the medium-term framework of macrocycles (several training weeks) it also requires a change in increasing, maintaining, and diminishing microcycles of stress (several training sessions).

That way excessive training demands can be avoided, and performance can be made to peak at specific times.

The circuit of international snowboarding competitions makes periodic and cyclical training absolutely indispensable at top levels of performance. But even at lower levels snowboarders should organize their training at least in the medium range, encompassing several weeks. As a general rule, even at the highest levels of performance no more than one or two workouts should be done in a single day. But at all levels it must be kept in mind that the ideal training situation is susceptible to interruption (by injury, for example), and that the snowboarder must once again adapt to different training conditions. ▬▬

Principle of Individuality and Age Appropriateness

This fundamental, which was just mentioned, should always be observed in relation to complex athletic ability, and it should be granted a secure place in every training plan. Identical performance results can be obtained by several athletes because of individual abilities that are weighted differently. So an athlete's individual circumstances should always be considered in order to produce the highest performance level.

It's appropriate to bring up the theme of riding style in relation to this principle. It's known that there are many ways to reach a goal. Snowboarders who have no leeway for their individual circumstances will never succeed in using their present chances and possibilities. The same is true with respect to age. Anyone who ignores age-related conditions is off the track to systematic progress. ■

With the division into preparation, competition, and transition periods, snowboarding training becomes increasingly specific in regard to discipline and highlights of the racing season. Overall conditioning training recedes in importance as preparation continues, and is increasingly replaced by on-snow training. ■

Principle of Diminishing Returns from Individual Training Elements

This principle refers to tailoring training to the athlete's conditioning and to the relationship between conditioning and technique training.

This is an important point for individual development for performance in any sport because various elements can have a positive and negative influence on one another.

In childhood and adolescence, races are an important motivating factor; enjoyment and fun should always be paramount.

In snowboarding, excessive endurance training can have a negative impact on coordination and speed. That's why careful structuring of year-round training is so important. While endurance training should definitely be an important part of transition periods, there is a shift in preparation and competition stages to developing performance-determining abilities (see Structure of Performance in Snowboarding Racing), and to techno-motor skills. ■

Principle of Increasing Specialization

In conjunction with specificity of stress stimulus, there is a difference between nonspecific and specific adjustments by the body. Specific adjustment applies in great measure to the immediately utilized organ system and is manifested locally, for example, in the skeletal musculature. As training progresses, this indicates an increasing amount of specific training and the priority of developing the abilities that determine performance.

Training Plans; Periodic and Cyclic Training

Training Plans

Planned training has been shown to be important in snowboarding competition. It is based on meaningful, individual setting of training goals and on methodical structuring of training controls and competitions. A training plan should exhibit increased adaptability and flexibility based on the rapid development of snowboarding. This concerns changes in rules and possible injuries in the course of the season (see Periodic and Cyclic Training).

Training plans are divided into long range (one year or multiyear), middle range (several months or weeks), and short range (monthly, weekly, or daily). They focus on the rider's development stage and cover the training levels from basic, developmental, and final up to high-performance training at the professional level.

Within the training plan a racer should undergo periodic training checks (see Fig. 6, p. 33) to determine present training condition. Possibilities include sport and techno-motor tests.

Training documentation forms the basis of the most effective overview of how training is progressing (see pp. 31 and 32). The documentation provides important information on the influence of changes in performance within specified time frames. The notes should always form the basis of a systematic plan and take into account athletic ability factors.

Phase Training

Phase training involves a change in training emphases (e.g., technique, methodology, and goals) with a view toward optimal performance. It is divided into what's known as the preparation phase with general and specific components; the competition phase (simple or complex); and the transition or recovery phase. All three comprise a periodic cycle.

At top levels of snowboarding it's possible to have multiple peaks in periodic training and in accompanying periodic cycles.

Fig. 3: Example of Phase Training with one, two, and three peaks

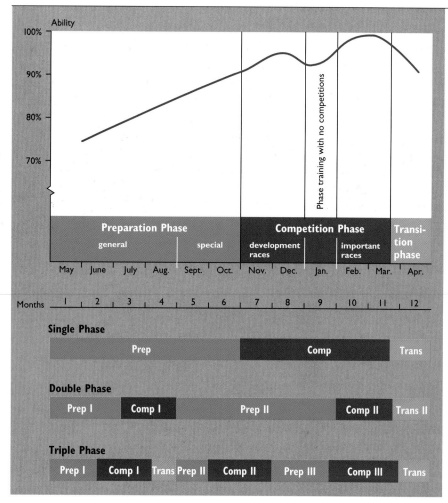

Cyclic Training

Cyclic training refers to organization of training time into sets of similar exercises, such as technique training. With regard to duration, we distinguish between
Workouts (WO): the smallest self-contained training element with subdivisions into warm-up, main part, and cooling-down
Microcycles (MIC): five to twelve workouts
Mesocycles (MEC): four to six weeks
Macrocycles (MAC): usually a periodic cycle

The so-called immediate preparation for competition (IPC) that takes place four to six weeks before a major event occupies a special place in the realm of mesocycles. Its content varies from rider to rider and depends on the particular discipline.

The so-called training content is divided into general exercises and developmental, sport- and competition-specific exercises.

Training unites specific training content with a type of exertion (e.g., riding intervals with incomplete pauses between). By training measures we mean ones that support training development. That way we can distinguish between organizational and informative measures (e.g., setting a course and explanation of movement, respectively), as well as equipment (e.g., short gate poles); see p. 58ff.

Training Methods

The basic goal of training is to enhance athletic performance. It is subject to individual conditions such as rebuilding after injury, and to goal setting.

Training methods include content of training, means of training, and method of applying exertion. Concepts taken from training methodology are of great importance in snowboarding.

In the realm of conditioning (see p. 14) there is a distinction among endurance, interval, repetition, and control methods. There are many variations within all of these.

In technique training, integral-, partial-, and integral-partial-integral methods have been formulated as a means of proceeding. These methods are not as clearly distinguishable from one another as in condition training.

Breaks should be consciously planned into training.

THE STRUCTURE OF PERFOR-MANCE IN SNOWBOARD RACING

Disciplines

In the course of the development of snowboard sports several disciplines have evolved both in Freestyle and in racing. In racing there are Giant Slalom, the Super G, and the Duel Slalom. In addition, in the winter of 1994–95 another discipline came about that incorporates elements from racing and Freestyle: Boardercross (see Freestyle).

The rapid development of disciplines has been evidenced also in rules changes. Until 1993 Giant Slalom and Super G were conducted with two long gate poles and a rectangular gate flag that was attached to the top third of the poles. Until the world cup season of 1995–96 Giant Slalom and Super G were run with one long and one short pole and a triangular gate flag attached to their lower portion. Given rapid development and changes, it's impossible to give an accurate prediction of rules that will govern individual disciplines in the future. But one thing is certain: the disciplines just mentioned will surely continue to be part of the snowboarding sport as time goes on.

The further growth in this sport, the trends, and the demands of snowboarders can surely create new disciplines.

Duel slalom racers experience immediate pressure from their opponent as well as technical demands.

In Giant Slalom and Super G riding dynamics and speed are key factors.

Boardercross races require lots of tactics in regard to opponents and choice of track.

Development

Before we delve directly into performance structure in snowboard racing, we should take a look at how racing started.

When snowboarding was becoming established, it was only a question of time before snowboarders would conduct competitions. Riding style and technique were not judged; what was judged was the fastest time down the course. No snowboarder had previously competed, and no one had done any preparation for the first races. Coping with the race course was based on the fundamental of trial and error. This development brought forth some talented snowboarders whose physical aptitudes corresponded to the requirements of the time. That allowed them to rise above the less talented "regular" snowboarders.

In the second phase of this development the "regular" snowboarders began to prepare for competition. The preparations were largely shaped by their collective experience and imaginativeness. As a result, even regular snowboarders suddenly were victorious over the more talented ones.

Purposeful race training was then undertaken by talented snowboarders, who soon were back in the winners' circle.

The race between very talented and less talented riders began and has continued to this day. The result of this development is today's snowboard training and the experiences connected to it.

Further development in riding technique will be shaped in the future by two essential factors. In the future the best talents will discover new solutions in conjunction with further developments in board materials. With the development of a new technique begins the process of evaluating its appropriateness to the overall training process of individual riders.

As everyone already knows, snowboarding as a competitive sport has come into its own with its inclusion in the 1998 Winter Olympic Games in Nagano, Japan. Audiences around the world enjoyed seeing this high-profile sport showcased in the media. Such coverage is sure to enhance snowboarding's following among individuals who enjoy new athletic challenges and ways to delight in winter sports.

As long as a new technique promises individual success, general training adjusts to the new conditions. There is no end in sight to this process.

Nevertheless, even in snowboard racing there are some basic factors that affect performance, forming the basis for the development just mentioned, and that will remain very important in the future.

The following view of performance structure is also a view of the riders' characteristics that influence performance. These natural abilities can be counted among them:

Well-developed elasticity and speed in combination with very good coordination

Given a view of performance structure in snowboard racing, the general model for complex athletic ability (see Fig. 1, p. 12) takes on a character specific to snowboarding. This should be examined more closely in conjunction with six performance factors. The factors analyzed are the basis of understanding

The biomechanical, physiological, and functional-anatomic conditions of movements and stresses in snowboarding, and the profile of conditioning, cognitive, psychological, anthropometric, social, and equipment requirements

In regard to the specific movements in snowboard racing, strength, speed, and agility are clearly more important than endurance. The motions involved in snowboard racing call for an especially large measure of elasticity. Because of the quick change between weighting and unweighting and between rapid edge changes, elasticity should be given lots of attention.

Endurance

Endurance in snowboarding is another important requirement among the skills that determine the racer's performance. It comes into play in qualification and final runs in keeping to a minimum the unavoidable loss of intensity experienced after riding the course. The extensive and varied stresses within the training process can also be better used if the rider has good endurance (fatigue resistance).

The most important factor in the rider's training process is quick recovery after training and competition. Well-developed endurance creates favorable conditions in the body.

In addition to basic endurance, discipline-specific endurance must be developed. Both types form the basis for endurance and elasticity in racing that lasts from thirty-five seconds to two minutes. Competitions are characterized by maximal stress intensity and partially anaerobic energy supply.

The development of a rider: Martin Freinadametz in 1988 and 1996; in addition to technique there are recognizable differences in equipment and gates.

The following profile of performance structure describes only some of the characteristics of snowboarding. It will serve as a stimulus for further refinement and clarification. The greater the detail of the profile as laid out by trainer or athlete, the clearer the training plans and their relations to one another.

Physical Performance Factors

Snowboard racing demands good conditioning on the rider's part. This becomes clear in the course of a competition where the rider has to go through several qualifications and final runs. The fundamental requirements of coping with this stress profile involve the athlete's general conditioning. The four conditioning skills of endurance, strength, speed, and agility should therefore be brought to a high level throughout the preparation period.

Strength

The muscular strength component is very important in racing. Strength demands on the rider are related to riding technique and style.

In snowboarding there are dynamic and static applications of the muscles (e.g., straightening legs in unweighting and schussing in a deep crouch). The dynamic use of the muscles can be positive, concentric, and forceful, or eccentric and decreasing (e.g., straightening legs in up-unweighting or moving downward in down-unweighting, respectively).

Strength is generally the basic requirement for a secure riding technique. Based on the asymmetrical position on the snowboard the rider's body can be divided into left and right sides in respect to muscular development. The main muscle groups used are

The hip and thigh muscles
The lower leg muscles and ankles
The muscles of the torso (spinal column)
The shoulder muscles

Toeside canting: concentric contraction of rear lower leg muscles with simultaneous straightening of front lower leg muscles.

Unweighting: short relaxation of both muscle areas during unweighting.

Heelside canting: concentric contraction of front lower leg muscles with simultaneous straightening of rear lower leg muscles.

Fig. 4: Workings and contraction patterns of muscles in the example of front and rear lower leg muscles while edging.

Muscle strength is based on muscle substance, and occurrences in the central and peripheral nervous system play a decisive role in muscle development. These occurrences are very important to coordination in snowboarding. They include

- Intramuscular coordination (nerves and muscles working together effectively within a specific movement, e.g., nerve-muscle interaction in thigh muscles for explosive up-unweighting)
- Intermuscular coordination (various muscles working together within a specific movement, e.g., interplay between back and hip muscles in a heelside turn)
- Preinnervation (activating the muscle before the actual strength requirement, as in preinnervation of the thigh muscle at the start of a turn)
- Reflex innervation (activating the muscle through the straightening reflex, as in a sudden balancing movement to avoid a fall or to correct a riding fault)

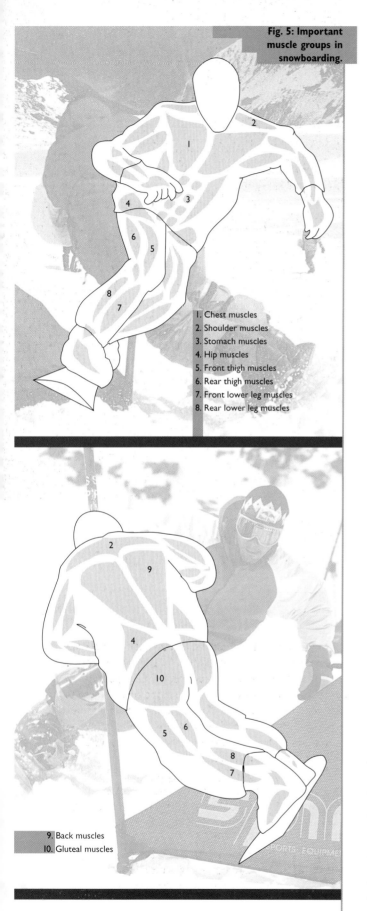

1. Chest muscles
2. Shoulder muscles
3. Stomach muscles
4. Hip muscles
5. Front thigh muscles
6. Rear thigh muscles
7. Front lower leg muscles
8. Rear lower leg muscles

9. Back muscles
10. Gluteal muscles

Within the various riding styles and techniques there are several important types of strength: elasticity, reactive strength, and submaximum strength endurance. Elasticity and reactive strength are especially important in trainability and training investment. They are trainable only to a certain extent, and are dependent upon the structure of the muscle fibers, that is, physical conditioning and talent. There is a distinction between fast-twitch or "white" muscle fibers (quick fibers), which are designed for elasticity, and slow-twitch "red" muscle fibers (slow fibers), which are used for endurance. There are also combinations of both types of fibers. Strength development takes a long time and should be started early.

In many types of snowboarding, well-developed elasticity is a very important element in performance. Specific movements, such as explosive unweighting, can be accomplished only through strength applied in a particular time frame. So the issue is quick movements accomplished at high contraction speeds. Elasticity in snowboarding makes possible very quick body movements, especially along the long body axis (vertical movements and weighting and unweighting).

Reaction strength, a particular form of elasticity, plays an important role in changing quickly between weighting and unweighting (see Fig. 9 p. 40), from one edge to the other (as on a narrow, steep course), or with sudden balancing movements to avoid a fall. Because of the resulting tensions, tendons and ligaments, as well as nerves and muscles, are important to performance.

An additional form that strength takes in snowboarding is endurance. It relates to the rider's resistance to fatigue in applying strength, and it depends on the extent to which it is applied.

These physical conditioning factors should not be considered in isolation, but in conjunction with one another. Riders who develop them to the fullest and combine them are likely to experience the greatest success. So endurance and strength become most useful to elite riders when combined with speed and mobility.

Speed

Speed is closely connected to the rider's elasticity and coordination. Speed is evident in virtually every phase of action and reaction time. Furthermore, it is fundamental to the rider's psychological abilities, including concentration and willpower.

Reaction time refers to the ability to respond to a stimulus in the shortest time possible. This type of speed occurs in several variations in training and competition. It's very important at the start or under fast changing surface conditions and is used to keep your balance when conditions change from granular to icy.

Long-term elasticity prevents loss of speed due to fatigue from muscular exertion. It is essential to continuous weighting and unweighting of the board for turning and steering over a specified time such as the duration of a run.

Agility

Agility is comprised of suppleness (movement of joints) and flexibility (stretchable quality of muscles).

As with all sports, snowbarding demands a special type of flexibility. Because of the asymmetrical position on the board flexibility is very important, and it serves a heightened protective function (see Stretching). Flexibility involves strong coordination as well as conditioning influences. It is a fundamental requirement for good technique and conditioning. Poor flexibility leads to

- Increased risk of injury
- Impaired learning of new movements
- Wasteful expenditures of energy
- Poor technique (e.g., interference with rhythm)

Technical and Coordination Performance Factors

In general there is a close connection between physical and technical-coordination performance factors. They should not be separated from one another. Elasticity is strongly influenced, as already mentioned, by coordination.

Special or sport-specific coordination abilities develop alongside riding technique. They are the most important performance factors in snowboard training and are a basic requirement for learning technical moves (good sensory and motor receptivity for learning). The higher the level of coordination, the quicker and more effectively difficult moves can be learned.

Rapid development of riding technique requires increased flexibility and adaptability of coordination in the rider. This becomes evident in a rapid and purposeful action such as quick edge changes.

Speed is important in racing, especially in high-speed hits, as in Giant Slalom. Quickness is needed at takeoff for a stable flight position.

The excellent riding technique of a top-level snowboarder is distinguished by its great economy of movement in precise steering. A top performer executes turns with a minimal expenditure of muscle force. In competition this amounts to important energy savings for the final run. The following functions of coordination are of paramount importance to snowboarders:

- Receiving and processing information through sense organs (e.g., early detection of a major bump on race course)
- Anticipation (mental anticipation) and programming of movement using available program of movements (e.g., high approach to gate)

Execution of appropriate muscle contractions (e.g., contraction of thigh muscle in unweighting) Continuous feedback on movement with simultaneous comparison between actual or theoretical execution and the intended movement (e.g., steering after anticipated downturn on suddenly encountered patch of ice)

There are five types of essential sensors that are responsible for motor coordination in snowboarding and that supplement one another:

Kinesthetic sensors are located in muscles, tendons, ligaments, and joints. They provide information about momentary body position and are responsible for fine tuning movements.

Tactile sensors are located on the skin; they provide information on form and snow surface conditions (e.g., by feeling condition of snow).

Static-dynamic sensors are located in the inner ear; they report on the head's direction and speed changes (e.g., rhythm change through gates).

Optical sensors make possible central and peripheral vision and provide information about movements (e.g., approaching a gate).

Acoustic sensors likewise provide information about movements by means of acoustic signals such as the noise of edges on ice.

One final important point relating to coordination in snowboard racers is their degree of practical experience in movement. Every snowboarder's goal should be to acquire as much practical movement experience as possible. That is the basis for the stringing together of distinct motions into a complete program of movement—an essential factor in snowboarding.

Psychological Performance Factors

Talent and technique contribute decisively to success in snowboard sports. But all too often those qualities are limited by a force that's stronger yet: the psyche. Racers who understand this component in their training can successfully approach their upper performance threshold.

In training and competition complex psychological stress factors arise; they include pressure to perform, long-lasting injuries, lack of success, deficient concentration, and fear of riding after a layoff due to injury. Further important factors are motivation, confidence, and self-discipline. A representative situation is waiting at the start, which can turn into a long process due to delays (using the new starting pairs in the KO system, or a false start by preceding pair). These are just a few examples of an endless quantity of factors that influence a rider's performance level. They shape athletes and are often the end of the line for their hard training. Psychological performance factors take on more significance than ever before given increases in performance levels. An essential point in this development is mental strength. That can be developed in many ways, and it holds the key to solving many types of problems.

In racing, concentration and desire bring success to a rider.

Equipment Factors

Equipment factors are part of the set of external conditions that snowboarders must deal with. Because of their importance they will be considered here separately.

The development of the board-binding-boot system is guided primarily by the racer's demands and requirements. New materials developed in response to racers' requirements have had a great impact on the development of riding technique. Here's an example: At first, even in racing, changes in direction were effected by turning the body. That was due largely to the slight degree of waisting and to the width of the board.

Because of further developments in snowboards those movements became less important in racing and could be diminished. New board technology naturally led to new emphases in today's riding technique: applying pressure to the edges and dynamic movement.

That's how the foregoing interaction between materials development and riding technique has come to have such a great effect on performance. The optimal match between materials and riders, with their adaptability to new riding techniques, is the result of the demands of today's racing.

A further aspect of equipment and material factors is protective gear. It too has been improved in recent years. Good protectors, gloves, and a light helmet (Giant Slalom and Super G) protect the body against long-lasting injuries, reduce anxiety, and offer optimal freedom of movement in training and competition. Here we should also mention the choice of gate pole material for training and competition: the proper pole material reduces danger of injury.

New board technology has contributed decisively to today's emphasis on technique, dynamics of movement, and buildup of pressure.

External Performance Factors

External performance factors are complex, and they greatly influence performance in training and competition. They should always be considered relative to tactical measures (e.g., proceeding with competition under poor visibility conditions) and to the psychological state of the rider (e.g., fear in steep terrain). Their variation is of great importance to the rider's training and improvement in technique.

The following factors related to weather, terrain, and regulations are especially important in snowboard racing:

Weather conditions

Temperature	**Warming up** **Waxing** **Riding technique**
Snow conditions	**Board preparation** **(Waxing, edge tuning)** **Riding technique** **Board choice**
Wind	**Riding technique**
Visibility	**Riding technique** **(most affective use of** **all sense organs)**

Terrain conditions

Pitch of slope and **ground conditions**	**Riding technique** **Board choice** **(length, waisting, etc.)**

Regulations

Discipline and **setting of course**	**Riding technique** **Board choice (length,** **profile, etc.)**

Bad weather conditions
are often a limiting factor
in race performance.

The influence of weather, terrain, and regulations on the rider's performance should decrease as training progresses. Further factors include opponents in a (slalom) run, spectators, the media, and the athlete's private life. All these areas have a positive or negative influence on the athletic ability of a snowboarder.

Tactical Performance Factors

Development of tactical competence is closely linked to the technical, conditioning, and psychological conditions of the rider and should be coordinated to them. Tactical competence is demonstrated in snowboard sports by board control and can always be developed further. Practical knowledge gained in this process can have a major effect on tactical measures. Tactics become increasingly important throughout the racer's training process.

Tactical measures in snowboard racing can be divided into four phases:

Intellectual understanding: All factors of athletic performance that have a measurable influence on the race are analyzed (e.g., inspecting the course to identify technical features).

Plan of action: A concept is formed to permit the rider to cope with the aforementioned conditions (e.g., quick and early edging in a narrow course).

Motor phase: In this phase the action plan is put into effect. That allows for changes in plan due to conditions (e.g., unexpected ice patches on the course that make edging difficult).

Analysis of results: Obtained results are evaluated subjectively, during and after the motor phase. Explanations are sought for any deviations and failures that occur (e.g., completion of the foregoing action plan for subsequent runs).

In the development of an accomplished racer the ability to anticipate becomes very important in the phases just outlined. It contributes significantly to developing a plan of action even in the face of disruptions, and it sets fine racers apart from the rest.

TRAINING PLANS

Planning Requirements

The fundamentals for training plans already set forth in Basics (see p. 12)—periodic and cyclic training—now need to be implemented on an individual basis. As already explained, the snowboarder should now objectively and realistically answer the following questions:

- What performance goals will be pursued?
- How much athletic ability does the rider possess?
- How much time is available for training?

These points are always connected to one another. That must be considered as they are clarified. Performance goals must correspond to the rider's athletic ability and to the available time.

In regard to time, professional, scholastic, and private obligations absolutely must be considered. Fluctuations in training time can be evened out with a training plan.

The training plan is based on the training principles described in detail under Basics. Those principles ensure a reliable and conclusive development through training. The training plan is an important part of managing performance (see p. 33).

Periodic and Cyclic Training

The organization of the year usually results in the preparation, competition, and transition periods mentioned earlier. But before a training program built on training principles and experience can begin, the following organizational points need to be explained. The effective number of training weeks and training hours should be calculated. Then determine the race dates. At top levels, that can be the most important step. Establishing preparation and transition periods follows from the race dates in the competition period. Usually competitions begin in November and end in April. They are set according to level by regional, national, or international races or race series. On the national level the national championships are the high point. In the international level

there are the World Championship, European Championship, and race series such as the World Pro Tour (WPT), which go on throughout the winter and which determine an overall champion. Starting in 1998, every four years the Winter Olympics provide another high point in the competitive season. It should also be noted that there are also competitions during the winter in the southern hemisphere. By planning for these competitions, races can be scheduled for the entire year.

This profusion of competitions underlines the urgency of a systematic training plan at all levels of performance (beginner, advanced, and world-class). That's usually the only way to ensure flexibility in case of postponed or canceled races. At top levels of snowboarding a long-term plan covering several years and with clearly defined goals should be adhered to.

If periodic training for an entire year is not practicable for beginners and advanced riders, training can be planned over a shorter period of time. In this case the available training weeks and hours are likewise calculated and the periodic training just explained is applied to that time period.

At the end of the plan standards and guidelines for objective performance evaluation are set (see Managing Performance). Actual training can then be matched to established goals by means of the standards.

Next begins the planning of micro- and mesocycles (MIC and MES, respectively). That is keyed to the all-important division of the year into various periods such as macrocycles (MAC). The greatest flexibility of the training plan exists within the microcycles (training weeks). It is advisable to keep a constant weekly microcycle schedule within a mesocycle (four to six weeks). That way training days of greater intensity can alternate with easier training days, according to the principle of optimal scheduling of stress and recovery. Consistent weekly patterns can promote recovery between workouts and reduce the level of stress that can arise in training plans that constantly change.

As the preparation period progresses, training intensity is increased progressively from mesocycle to mesocycle until it is maximized during the competition period (see Fig. 3, p. 18). At the same time the recovery level should also be increased. The intensity profile within mesocycles can be set up in different ways, but it must correspond to the stress-recovery principle. For example, the intensity can be slowly increased within microcycles until the next-to-the-last week (building weeks). In the last week of training, the intensity of workouts should be reduced dramatically in anticipation of the greatly increased stresses in the following mesocycle. The idea is to build in sufficient recovery and adjustment to the training load.

A further example involves "hard" weeks that alternate with more relaxed weeks of reduced intensity. A limitless number of variations are possible; in any case, they must be adapted to the fundamental training principles. The most important thing is to experiment with the many variables and to decide empirically what works best for individual riders.

In the course of the winter it can happen that a number of competitions are scheduled within the same week (or microcycle). In such cases, planning and organization are of the utmost importance. Without such forethought fatigue, logistical and transportation problems, and inadequate preparation will be reflected in race results, and perhaps even in the rider's physical and mental state. The effects of a negative experience may be felt for the remainder of the season, perticularly if the rider has to deal with diminished confidence or with physical injury. The following example of a week that contains several competitions will make it clear how planning and organization can be used to optimize a competitor's chances for success in a week of intensive competition:

Essential Organizational Goals of a Training Plan

Calculating all training weeks and training hours

Setting competition dates

Setting preparation and transition periods

Setting objective standards and guidelines to control training

Planning macro-, meso-, and microcycles

ONE WEEK / SEVEN DAYS

Travel from previous competition or workout to race location
Hotel registration and subsequent equipment preparation for following race day

1. Overnight

Qualification runs for Duel Slalom and equipment preparation for next day

2. Overnight

Competition in Giant Slalom with subsequent awarding of prizes and press conference; then equipment preparation for following day

3. Overnight

Competition in Duel Slalom with subsequent awarding of prizes and press conference; then equipment preparation and transfer to next race site

4. Overnight

Riding workout followed by equipment preparation for race on following day

5. Overnight

Competition in Giant Slalom with subsequent awarding of prizes and press conference, preparation of equipment for next day

6. Overnight

Qualification runs for Duel Slalom and equipment preparation for following day

7. Overnight

Duel Slalom competition followed by awarding of prizes and press conference, equipment preparation, and departure

Table 1. Training Plan for the Year

	Name	
I	Disciplines and Competitions	
2	Performance Goals	
3	Physical Preparation	
4	Psychological Preparation	
5	Technical Preparation	
6	Tests and Standards	

Table 2.

Weekly Plan

Days	Conditioning Training				Technique Training general		Technique Training special			Develop-ment races	Important races	Observa-tions
	Endurance	Strength	Speed	Agility	Other sports	Freeriding	SL	GS	Super G			
1. Monday												
2. Tuesday												
3. Wednesday												
4. Thursday												
5. Friday												
6. Saturday												
7. Sunday												
Number of hours												

Total number of hours in week: ....

Table 3. Competitions

Comp. No.	Date	Sponsor	Discipline	Outside Conditions	Performance Time, Place	Comments
1						
2						
3						
4						
5						
6						
etc.						

Table 4. Personal Evaluation

EMPHASIS	positive	negative	
Conditioning			
Endurance			
Strength			
Speed			
Agility			
Overall Coordination			
Riding Technique			
PSYCHOLOGICAL STATE			
In Training			
In Competition			

MANAGING PERFORMANCE

Before snowboarders start training they should take stock of their current performance. This applies to beginners as well as to top-level athletes—for example, after a fairly long layoff due to injury. The road to high performance as an individual is usually long and hard. It must always be undertaken with repeated, systematic, and methodical steps. Individual steps are oriented to the performance of the rider, to knowledge gained from training, and to universal fundamentals of training science.

The resulting habits are regarded as a means to direct performance. In the process of managing performance the individual factors of complex athletic skills are developed to a maximum. The basis for this control process is a detailed knowledge of performance structure.

The following model for performance management according to Grosser applies to snowboarding as well as to other sports. The entire training process is based on this model and clarifies the inter-relationships of the planning steps in all training.

Phase 1: At the start of training, beginners and advanced racers alike (e.g., after layoffs due to injury) analyze their training state (athletic ability analysis).

Phase 2: In the second phase, the short- and long-term individual performance goals and norms are formulated as guidelines (e.g., determined course times for train-ing). At the same time, training phases and competition dates within a year are coordinated (periodic training).

Phase 3: The third phase involves the actual training and competitions.

Phase 4: In the fourth phase the training performances (e.g., course times for various types of tasks) are controlled as much as possible and the competition results are consulted as independent control parameters (see Tables 1-4, pp. 31-32). Further recommended control measures include videotaping training and competition and recording times in training runs.

Phase 5: The last phase within performance management involves immediate evaluation of the control parameters. They are useful in sticking to a plan of action.

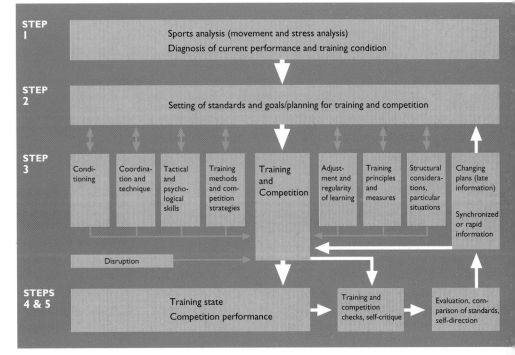

Fig. 6: Model for managing and regulating athletic performance in snowboard training and competition, adapted from Grosser.

CONDITIONING TRAINING

Conditioning training in snowboarding seeks to improve both general and specific conditioning. General conditioning training addresses steady development of the heart and circulatory system, muscle strength, and flexibility. It is also the basis for snowboarding-specific conditioning training (see Performance Factors) in the preparation and competition periods. Snowboarding-specific conditioning training is closely bound to technique training and includes the combined conditioning and coordination skills in training plans. The chapter entitled Technique Training (p. 48) is of particular importance in regard to systematic measures and in carrying out this training.

Overall conditioning training is subject to the training principles mentioned earlier (see p. 13) and to the model for managing performance (p. 33).

Given the complex adaptation processes and requirements, more complete professional literature should be referred to for this.

By the middle of the preparation period, general endurance should be at a very high level, since it is important for the rest of the training. It should also be concluded by at least that time because of its importance to other emphases as periodic training progresses, such as technique training in the preparation and competition periods. Training for the speed and endurance typically needed in racing is accomplished mainly during the preparation period, but also in the competition period. One should always be aware that endurance training can be a limiting factor in elasticity and speed.

Endurance Training

The idea of endurance training for snowboarders is improvement of the points made in the section entitled Physical Performance Factors (endurance).

Because of the increasing importance of riding dynamics, conditioning plays an ever greater role in determining performance in snowboard racing.

Training Methods

The following methods have proven their worth in endurance training for snowboarding:

- Duration Training
- Interval Training
- Repetition Training

Duration Training (see Fig. 7) uses continuous, productive stresses, such as running at a constant speed. There is a distinction between continuous (constant stress level), variable (scheduled changes in stress), and irregular (random changes in stress and speed play) duration methods. The goal is enhanced functioning of the organ systems, such as increasing the capacity of the heart and circulatory system.

The Interval Method (see Fig. 7) is characterized by scheduled changes between stress phases and relaxation phases. By relaxation we mean incomplete, productive breaks. The type of break depends on the individual rider's conditioning and on the intensity and the duration of stress. The criterion for judging recovery is the heart rate (120–130 beats per minute). Interval methods are distinguished according to intensity (extensive or intensive) and by duration of stress (short intervals of 15–60 seconds; medium intervals lasting from one to three minutes; and long intervals of three to eight minutes). When training is done in sets involving four to six repetitions, longer breaks between sets are called for.

The repetition method is characterized by repeated intense to extremely intense stresses with alternating complete recovery periods where heart rate drops to fewer than 100 beats per minute. In all instances performance parameters return to the starting condition.

All training methods should include stretching at beginning and end (see agility). That avoids shortening of muscles and protects against injuries.

Fundamentals of General Endurance Training

Basic endurance training generally should be conducted over a three-month time frame (transition periods and preparations periods) in a yearlong training period. Within the competition period it comes into use predominantly as warm-up and recovery measures (e.g., relaxed easing off).

For overall endurance, training sports like running, cycling, swimming, and in-line skating are appropriate. They make possible a continuous and fairly long-lasting exertion. The intensity is controlled by speed of motion. For precision, the heartbeat (aerobic and anaerobic) should be monitored.

Training frequency depends on the goals set by the individual. Many times the program can be conducted with other sports that match the stress profile just given. A program of an hour per weekend and one to two supplementary sessions of about fifteen minutes each is the bare minimum. Optimizing the points addressed in The Structure of Performance in

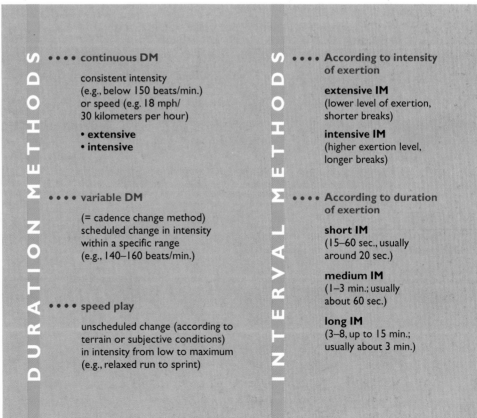

DURATION METHODS

•••• **continuous DM**

consistent intensity
(e.g., below 150 beats/min.)
or speed (e.g. 18 mph/
30 kilometers per hour)

- **extensive**
- **intensive**

•••• **variable DM**

(= cadence change method)
scheduled change in intensity
within a specific range
(e.g., 140–160 beats/min.)

•••• **speed play**

unscheduled change (according to
terrain or subjective conditions)
in intensity from low to maximum
(e.g., relaxed run to sprint)

INTERVAL METHODS

•••• **According to intensity of exertion**

extensive IM
(lower level of exertion,
shorter breaks)

intensive IM
(higher exertion level,
longer breaks)

•••• **According to duration of exertion**

short IM
(15–60 sec., usually
around 20 sec.)

medium IM
(1–3 min.; usually
about 60 sec.)

long IM
(3–8, up to 15 min.;
usually about 3 min.)

Fig. 7: Variations in Duration
and Interval Methods
according to Zintl.

Showboard Racing chapter would be most desirable; that should not, however, involve other combined conditioning and coordination skills (e.g., speed). Consequently, training should include extensive and intensive intervals (e.g., sprints over 40 yards/meters).

General endurance training need not become tedious or monotonous. Any athletic activity that increases heart rate and lung capacity is appropriate. For variety's sake, change activities and train with other people.

Mountain biking in the summertime is best suited to improving endurance and strength endurance.

Speed Endurance Training

Speed endurance training becomes increasingly important in the course of the preparation period. It improves the energy supply in the muscles per time unit, normal lactic acid build-up, and levels of speed and strength.

Furthermore, intermuscular coordination and the level of psychological activation (distribution of stress hormones) needs to be developed in snowboarding-specific speed endurance training. The training is closely tied to specific strength training (see p. 41).

Interval and repetition methods come into play in speed endurance. The following are measures that can be used for specific speed endurance training:

- Riding a tight Giant Slalom course
- Riding several short slalom runs that are set up one after another on a single course
- Riding a course set up with varying distances between gates
- Taking several runs in succession without a break

Strength Training

Strength training is also subject to extremely complex physiological and anatomical interrelations (see Fig. 8) that are beyond the scope of this chapter. Just the same, the training principles (see p. 13) still apply. The following questions should be answered before training begins:

- What are the objectives of strength training (e.g., rebuilding after injury, or elasticity at top levels of competition)?
- What aspects should be developed (e.g., strength endurance or speed)?
- What kind of strength improvement is desired (e.g., muscle growth)?
- Is there a type of strength training that corresponds to riding technique (e.g., training with joints at specific angles)?

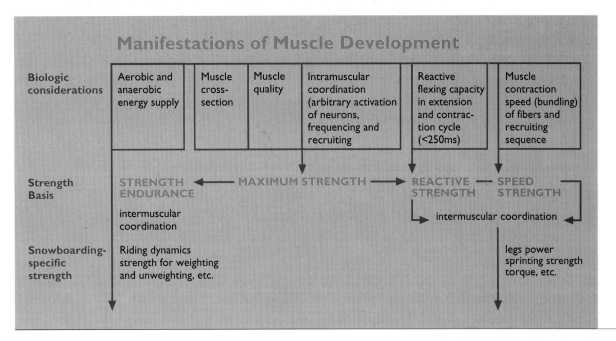

Manifestations of Muscle Development						
Biologic considerations	Aerobic and anaerobic energy supply	Muscle cross-section	Muscle quality	Intramuscular coordination (arbitrary activation of neurons, frequencing and recruiting	Reactive flexing capacity in extension and contraction cycle (<250ms)	Muscle contraction speed (bundling) of fibers and recruiting sequence
Strength Basis	STRENGTH ENDURANCE ←			MAXIMUM STRENGTH →	REACTIVE STRENGTH —	SPEED STRENGTH
	intermuscular coordination				intermuscular coordination	
Snowboarding-specific strength	Riding dynamics strength for weighting and unweighting, etc.					legs power sprinting strength torque, etc.

Fig. 8: Manifestations of muscle development and strength, modified according to Grosser.

Training Methods

Training methods are keyed to the objectives mentioned earlier and to the strength properties that need to be developed. The strength training method is precisely defined by concrete details of individual stress components. The following abbreviations help clarify the individual stress components:

```
MW:  How the muscles work;
concentric, eccentric (see
Performance Structure/Strength)
I: Intensity of stress; this is
determined by the load (L) and
the movement speed (MS). The
following levels apply to maximum
load (ML): maximum (100-90%);
submaximum (90-80%); medium
(80-70%); light (70-50%);
minimal (50-30%)
S: Set: e.g., three times twelve
repetitions of the same exercise
(three sets of twelve reps with a
break of X minutes between sets)
D: Duration of an exercise (set);
expressed in time or number of
repetitions (NR)
B: Break of specified duration
SB: Break between sets
RB: Rest break between individual
exercises
R: Range; expressed in number of
sets
```

There are various types of strength training to choose from. The choice depends on one's objectives. The following types of training, which are presented without further explanation, can be useful:

■ Free exercises
■ Vaulting
■ Medicine ball
■ Wall bars
■ Cables
■ Weight vests
■ Sandbags
■ Dumbbells
■ Barbells
■ Strength training machines
■ Electrotherapy devices

Strength training can be done as station training, series training, or circuit training.

With station training, complete sets of an exercise are completed one after another at the same station. Series training consists of several sets, where a set is comprised of two to five exercises. These exercises are done one after another, before starting the next series. In circuit training several exercise stations (more than five) are completed in succession.

To avoid injury (muscle pulls and tears) and to promote better training, every type of muscle strength training should include a warm-up of at least fifteen minutes.

To avoid muscle shortening as a result of usage, stretching is an absolutely essential part of strength training.

Every training session should end with a cooling down, such as a relaxed run or stretching exercises.

General Strength Training

Basic training is important to overall strength development. It provides the foundation for the training for maximum strength and elasticity that are so important in snowboarding. The goal of training is an increase in muscle cross-section.

Overall strength training (muscle building) takes on special significance in snowboarding. Because of the asymmetrical stance and the attendant asymmetrical demands on the muscles (e.g., of the back), basic training has not only a developmental but also a preventive role in avoiding major injuries.

This calls for exercises (see Mobility Training) within the entire training process. They can also help in rebuilding the muscles after injury.

General strength training is appropriate for beginners as well as for up-and-coming racers, or for direct preparation for speed and elasticity training. It therefore should be tailored to every objective.

Added muscle strength and flexibility aid performance in part because they keep riders training longer and more effectively. Combined with warmups and stretching they avoid down time due to injuries.

The following **METHODS OF MUSCLE BUILDING** have distinct objectives. They refer to overall strengthening of the musculature or to strengthening the muscle groups important in snowboarding (see Performance Structure/Strength), and to complex strength development. Muscle development is conducted in the first eight weeks of training—the preparation period. It provides the basis for further strength training. Neglecting this training not only hinders performance but also increases risk of injury. Layoffs due to injury prolong this period. According to individual performance level, a different method can be selected from the following list in accordance with training principles:

MW:	How the muscles work
I:	Intensity of stress
L:	Load
MS:	Movement speed
ML:	Maximum load
S:	Set
D:	Duration of an exercise
NR:	Number of repetitions
B:	Break of specified duration
SB:	Break between sets
RB:	Rest break
R:	Range

METHODS with minimal strength requirements and medium to high numbers of repetitions (youth or development training, equilibrium training, and rebuilding after injury)
Muscle groups: entire movement system; MW: concentric, I: minimal; L: 30–50%; MS: slow to quick; NR: 10–100; S: 2–5; 8–15 exercises; B: 1–3 minutes between sets

METHODS with light strength requirements with medium number of repetitions (training for beginners, for development after injury)
Muscle groups: entire movement system. MW: concentric; I: medium; L: 45–65%; MS: quick; D: 50% of maximum repetition, approx. 8–15 NR; P: 1–3 minutes without complete recovery; R: high, 6–8 sets for every 3–4 exercises.

With these methods simple exercises are available that can be done in a full range of movement. After about twenty to twenty-five workouts the exercises should be changed.

The number of repetitions and the load should be increased gradually (see Training Principles).

DEVELOPING fast-twitch muscles in preparation for speed and elasticity training (beginners, advanced juniors, advanced racers, and top-level racers)

```
Muscle groups: snowboard specific
musculature (see Fig. 5, p. 24 or
Performance Structure/Strength).
MW: concentric; I: medium; L: 30—50%;
MS: as fast as possible; D: 10—30
NR or 15—40 sec.; B: 2 min. and
longer. R: 2—5 sets for every 3—6
exercises.
```

If the tempo of the exercise slows down perceptibly, the set should be interrupted; otherwise the slow-twitch muscles will be trained. Movements must be carried out in just the right way.

Complex Strength Development

Sequels to muscular development training include training for maximum strength, elasticity, and reaction strength, the last two of which are closely tied to maximum strength. Complex development of muscle strength targets the hip and upper and lower leg muscles, along with simultaneous application of strength training for the remaining muscle groups (prevention). Complex development of muscle strength in the legs is an important determining factor in snowboarding (see Performance Structure/Strength).

The most important ways to develop leg strength should therefore be mentioned here. The following types of training (maximum strength and elasticity training) should be applied alternately or in parallel after buildup of maximum strength in the preparation period. Let's emphasize once again the importance of good general strength development as it applies to complex strength demands of snowboarding. If this fundamental requirement is neglected there is an elevated risk of injury in the following types of training.

A dynamic riding technique presupposes optimal development of snowboarding-specific muscle groups such as back, hip, and upper leg musculature.

Maximum Strength Training:
Maximum strength is defined as the greatest strength that can be voluntarily produced against an insurmountable resistance. It takes precedence over elasticity and reactive strength and meets their basic requirements. Maximum strength depends in great measure on

```
Muscle cross section
Intramuscular coordination
```

The following important methods apply to snowboard training:

```
METHODS of exhaustive submaximum strength
```
application (hypertrophy methods)
```
MW: concentric—steady; I: submaximum;
L: 80-90% (variants 70% and 95%);
MS: slow to quick; D: to temporary
```

local muscular exhaustion, approx. 5–10 NR (variation: 3–18); about 20–30 sec.; B: 3–5 min.; SB: in set training 2–3 min. between stations; R: high, 5–10 sets per exercise (approx. 80–120 individual reps per muscle group over 2–3 exercises)

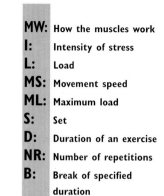

METHODS of explosive maximum strength application (methods of intramuscular coordination, IC methods)

MW: concentric; I maximum; L: 90–100%; MS: quick, with explosive strength; D: 1–5 NR; B: 3–5 min.; R: 5–12 sets per exercise (approx. 30–50 individual reps per muscle group with two exercises)

COMBINATION METHODS (Pyramid methods, see Fig. 9)

In pyramid methods, hypertrophy and IC methods are combined. Sets with hypertrophy effect (pyramid base) are complemented by sets of IC effect (pyramid tip). The entire range consists of nine to twelve sets and should represent an intensity between submaximum (hypertrophy methods) and maximum (IC methods) loads.

Elasticity and Reactive Strength Training:

As already made clear in Performance Structure in Snowboard Racing, elasticity is of the greatest importance in snowboarding. It should therefore receive ample attention in training. A close corollary is reactive strength, which will not be addressed separately, but rather treated as a complement to elasticity training. The basic requirements of training with the following methods consist of satisfactory completion of the training areas just mentioned. The following are central to training:

- Hypertrophy (growth) of fast-twitch muscle fibers
- Intermuscular coordination
- Optimum development of intramuscular coordination, or improving contraction speed
- Development of reactive tension strength
- Intermuscular coordination (relative to riding technique)

The following training methods arise from these important objectives:

1x	95%		80%	4x	
2x	90%		85%	3x	
3x	85%	**b**	90%	2x	
4x	80%	4x	95%	1x	
5x	75%	5x	95%	1x	
	70%	6x	90%	2x	
	65%	7x	85%	3x	
a	60%	8x	80%	4x	**c**

Fig. 9: Three distinct variations in pyramid methods: a, normal pyramid; b, truncated pyramid; c, double pyramid

TRAINING FOR MUSCLE STRESS

MW: concentric; I: minimal; L: 30–60%; MS: fast, explosive; D: 6–8 NR, cut short if MS or maximum impulse cannot be sustained; B: SB of 3–5 min.; recovery breaks of 5–10 sec.; R: minimal, 6–10 sets

REACTIVE STRENGTH TRAINING

```
MW: eccentric-concentric;
I: maximum-supramaximum; L: none, or
minimal; MS: maximum; D: 8—10 NR;
B: 5—12 min.; SB: approx. 5 sec.;
RB, R: minimal, 3—5 sets
```

Stress should be increased very slowly in reactive strength training. Hip exercises for one and both legs are included at the start of training for the benefit of the leg extension muscles. Later these are replaced by jumps over low hurdles and then by high jumping.

Snowboarding-specific Strength Training

Special strength training for racing seeks to create development of both strength endurance and elasticity. This last is closely connected to development of speed (see p. 43). The use and scope of these measures depends on the performance level of the individual rider. The given times and numbers are therefore only reference points and can vary greatly.

Snowboarding-specific Strength Endurance Training:

Snowboarding-specific strength endurance training is based on general strength training. It builds on the latter and combines it with development of discipline-specific movement. Training refers to the snowboarding-specific speed endurance mentioned earlier. The number of runs depends heavily on the individual performance level, the snow conditions, and the course. The following systematic measures can be applied:

```
Long training runs (in Giant
Slalom approx. 1.5 min. long;
in Slalom, approx. 40-50 gates;
training should be conducted on
trails served by chair lifts to
provide adequate and effective
rest breaks)
Training under difficult snow
conditions with normal course
lengths
Training on very soft surface:
riding the trough
```

Elasticity and reactive strength are especially important in unweighting.

Riding the trough offers the best opportunities to improve snowboarding-specific strength endurance.

Snowboarding-specific Elasticity Training:

Snowboarding-specific elasticity training is built upon general elasticity training. The complexity of the workout is closely connected to snowboarding-specific technique training. Basic training pertains to improvement of

```
Discipline-specific coordination
Reaction speed
```

41

Improvement of both factors contributes to greater speed in individual movements and to overall quickness. In the framework of discipline-specific coordination speed, the cycle of muscle extension and flexion and movement speed are improved. In the realm of reaction time, simple, situational reactions are encouraged, and so-called reaction options (i.e., choice of movement appropriate to a given situation) are improved.

The following measures are applicable to this training:

- Discipline-specific variations in setting the course
- Short runs requiring highest possible frequency of movement
- Slalom training with pro-jumps
- Training runs (about 100 yds./meters in length) on specially prepared camel humps

Further measures will be provided in the section on Speed Training (see p. 43).

Periodic and Cyclic Training

Strength training in snowboarding depends on periodic divisions. A half-year period is usual for strength training. With multiple periods in the entire training process, strength training has to fit into these conditions. The following deals with a season divided into simple periods:

The **PREPARATION PERIOD** is divided into two stages.

In the first stage of about eight weeks, general strength training is conducted. This provides the physical and psychological conditions required for higher demands in the future. At this training stage, individual muscle groups can be emphasized in accordance with the athlete's physical requirements. The second stage of the preparation period is characterized by clear specialization in muscle stresses specific to snowboarding. Maximum strength training and elasticity training are incorporated emphatically into the training program. The scope of strength training stays the same, but intensity is increased gradually. The second stage likewise comprises about eight weeks. At the end of this stage the rider should be at the previous year's performance level.

In the subsequent **COMPETITION PERIOD** the scope of training is reduced somewhat. But it is conducted at considerably higher intensity, allowing for individual differences. The high intensities are applied directly to on-snow training (technique

training). According to the length of the competition period, this portion can last up to three months. At this point the accompanying balance training needs to be emphasized again.

In the **TRANSITION PERIOD** (approximately five to eight weeks) a complete recovery of strength occurs. Through active recovery in other sports and reduced general strength training, a major reduction in performance level is avoided.

Deviations from these structures jeopardize the entire training program. A snowboard racer who carries on muscle development training during the competition period is out of synch with the requirements of that period, which call for maximum speed. Strength training is effective only if applied at the right time. The following time frames have proved appropriate:

- Muscle development training: four to eight weeks
- Hypertrophy training: four to five weeks
- Intramuscular training: three to five weeks
- Elasticity training: three weeks

Another essential point for effective structuring of strength training involves the meso- and micro-cycles.

The mesocycle consists of four to eight weeks in the preparation period, and three to four weeks in the competition period. It involves changes in stress level.

The microcycle (seven days) is characterized by continuous changes in scope and intensity (see Training Plans). Effective strength training depends on an understanding of the close relationship between exertion and recovery. This interrelation is of great importance in planning the microcycle.

Workouts in the microcycle can turn into definite objectives. Effects of overcompensation (see Training Principles) can also arise in strength training as a result of high-stress stimulus applied two to three days before race date. Micro- and mesocycles in strength training should always be controlled with a view to better management.

A workout in strength training should always be divided into warm-up, main part, and cooling-down phases. The following should be considered in planning training for technique and conditioning:

- Special conditioning before general conditioning
- Speed before strength
- Strength before endurance
- Technique training before conditioning training

Speed Training

Speed is considered a psychophysical ability. It is comprised of the four dimensions described in Fig. 10 and always appears in conjunction with a component of athletic performance. It is visible only at maximum effort in the absence of fatigue. The decisive limiting factor is fatigue. In physical abilities this refers to loss of energy during activity.

Speed is closely connected to strength. Maximum strength, elasticity, and speed should be regarded as a single unit in training. A large part of strength training turns into speed training. This training and its methods were presented in detail earlier. The following fundamental of speed training is a product of that context:

The fastest possible movements can be developed only through training exercises carried out at the highest possible speed. If training runs or training exercises are conducted too frequently at submaximum instead of maximum intensity, movements will actually slow down through building of slow-twitch muscle fibers.

This fact should also be considered in periodic training.

Management of the elasticity muscles depends heavily on psychological and neuronal activation (intermuscular coordination). The fatigue factor also plays a decisive role here through central nervous system fatigue.

Complex speed training is conducted in snowboarding in the course of the preparation and the competition periods with technique training (see p. 48). Here the anticipation, which is so important to speed, is improved. As psychological control or mental fitness develops in the entire training process, intake and processing of information are perfected.

This leads effectively to a faster performance of movement. In the psychological realm, heightened concentration and willpower are decisive requirements for development of speed.

The ideas of M. Grosser relative to motor speed are summarized in the following table. While a few factors (such as age and sex) are beyond our control, the reader will be struck by the large number of contributing elements over which we can exert some influence, and which are subject to training. This chart includes both physical and psychological factors and points to the need for balanced training. While some feel that biology is destiny in terms of performance, the following summary indicates that there is indeed plenty that all riders can work on to develop their ability to perform.

Fig. 10: Dimensions comprising motor speed, according to Grosser.

Dimensions of aptitude, development, snd learning	Sensory, cognitive, and psychological dimensions	Neuronal dimensions	Tendon/muscle dimensions	
Sex	Concentration (selective attention)	Selecting and frequencing motor units (= intramuscular coordination)	Distribution of muscle fiber types	S
Talent			Cross-section area of FT-fibers	P
Constitution	Receiving and processing information, management, and control	Stimulation and relaxation change in the ZNS (=inter-muscular coordination)	Muscle contraction speed	E
Age			Muscle-tendon elasticity	E
Athletic technique (quality)		Speed in conveying stimuli	Flexibility (viscosity)	D
Anticipation of movement	Motivation, will-power, readiness for exertion	Preinnervation	Muscle length and leverage of extremities and body	
		Reflex innervation	Energy supply	
			Muscle temperature	

Reaction speed is of
paramount importance
in tight courses.

- Speed and precision
- Fatigue
- Pretensing of muscles
- Preperiods ("Presignals")
- Goal orientation

Reaction games involving catching and kicking, and starts in various body positions upon acoustic and visual signals, are useful in general reaction training. At first training conditions are easy, and then more difficult or variable.

The exercises require that the rider be well rested. Rest periods are active, for instance, with easy jogging, and last two to three minutes before starting the next exercise. Within a workout no more than ten exercises should be done.

Special reaction training is part of technique training. It starts in the second half of the preparation period and is emphasized in competition period training. Various conditions are created within the training runs for technique training. In these training methods the already familiar training principles must be carefully observed. Any excessive demands on the racer's part could have disastrous effects on the rest of the training process, such as a bad fall under difficult conditions.

Reaction Speed

Snowboard racing places great demands on reaction speed because of its fast-changing situations. For that reason we should have a closer look at training for reaction speed. Further speed training is closely bound to technique training and will be addressed in that section.

REACTION PERFORMANCE in snowboarding is influenced by the following dimensions:

- Intensity of stimulus
- Age and sex
- Posture and body parts employed
- Environmental components and warmth (warming up)
- Number of reaction alternatives

Training in varying
conditions such as
soft snow and poor
visibility is an
opportunity to improve
reaction speed.

The following **MEASURES** are appropriate to this type of training:

- Training under varying snow conditions
- Riding courses with troughs
- Riding under poor visibility
- Setting up courses in different ways

These methods specifically heighten alertness and sensory motor activity, and they help the racer acquire differentiated types of movement. In artificially produced situations, an expert will react to select the correct type of movement.

Mobility Training

A snowboarder's mobility consists of suppleness (mobility in the joints) and flexibility in muscles, tendons, and ligaments. It is of great importance in movement. In the training process it should therefore be subject to constant controls.

Mobility is a mixed conditioning-coordination ability. It comes from the following **FACTORS THAT INFLUENCE AND LIMIT PERFORMANCE:**

- Anatomic and biomechanical correlations
- Muscular and neurophysiological limitations
- Age and development
- Psychological makeup
- Environmental influences
- Conditioning
- Fatigue
- Warm-up

The extreme importance of mobility training becomes clear if it is left out of the training program (see Performance Structure in Freestyle). **INSUFFICIENT MOBILITY** produces

- Increased danger of injury
- Difficulty in learning new movements
- Wasteful energy expenditure
- Inadequate performance of technique

A rider's mobility is an essential factor in the dynamics of movement in riding technique.

There is another reason why mobility training is important in overall training. It forms the transition from rest to stress and prepares the body physically and psychologically for imminent workouts or competition. Later on it provides physically and psychologically harmonious cooling-down at the conclusion of training and competition.

A stretching program for overall mobility is basic to mobility training. It is not subject to isolation in its own period, but should be conducted all-yearlong. It must be adjusted to training and competition demands and increased as appropriate. Individual programs can be formulated according to ample sports literature (e.g., Anderson). Here the stretching methods enumerated in Fig. 11 come into play.

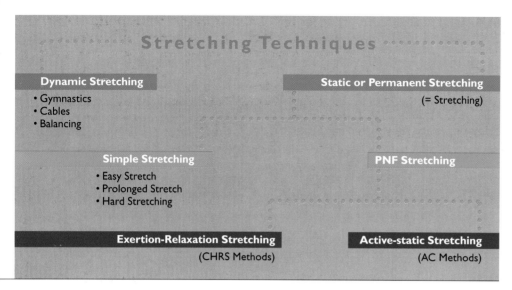

Fig. 11: Overview of various stretching techniques. PNF = Proprioceptive Neuromuscular Facilitation (lightening of stretching under use of reflex circuits, which come from proprioceptors, i.e., muscle or joint pivots); CHRS = Contract-Hold-Relax-Stretch; AC = Antagonist Contraction

Stretching

In stretching, the stretch position of the applicable muscle group is assumed slowly and carefully for fifteen to thirty seconds. Then relax the muscle perceptibly (Easy Stretch). Afterward the stretching position is carefully strengthened and once again held for the same duration (Development Stretch).

In this way each muscle group is stretched three to five times. After each stretch, change to different or opposing muscle groups (e.g., left/right thigh muscles).

Exertion-Relaxation Stretching

In this method a strong isometric contraction of about five seconds is applied before stretching. This involves muscle effort against insurmountable resistance without changing the length of the muscle.

After its sudden release in the final phase of stretching, the stress produces and supports what's called self-restraint in the muscle. The technique is used with three to five repetitions.

Active-Static Stretching

With this method, an antagonistic muscle is contracted (i.e., a muscle that counteracts the muscle in use). This produces a restraint (reciprocal antagonistic blocking) on the muscle subjected to stretching.

This method is not applicable to all muscle groups. It depends heavily on the bone structure of the joints. This is similar to both of the preceding methods.

Imbalance Stretching

The asymmetrical movements on the snowboard mentioned earlier make absolutely essential a specific stretching program for snowboarding-specific synergistic and antagonistic muscle groups (cooperating and opposing muscles, respectively; see Performance in Freestyle), particularly in respect to possible injuries resulting from excessive muscular imbalance. That should be implemented in conjunction with general strength training (Imbalance-Strength Training). Imbalance stretching is integrated into the general stretching program. It is distinguished by the increased number of stretching repetitions and by its application to the snowboarding-specific muscle groups.

This program should be adapted to the respective periods and to overall stress. During the competition period its scope should be expanded to correspond to the high stresses.

Fall Training

A special form of mobility training is fall training. Risk of injury in falls cannot be eliminated.

Since special on-snow fall training is not possible due to heightened risk of injury, a specific training for improving fall coordination and mobility in other sports should be conducted. The following sports and methods are appropriate:

- Judo
- Minitrampoline
- Jumping with minitrampoline on soft mat
- Water bounding

Systematic measures constitute improving and making automatic rolling and rotation movements. They should be practiced extensively in the transition and preparation periods. The complexity of the movements should be increased as training goes on, since they are important injury prevention measures.

Fall training can also help with recovery in races.

TECHNIQUE TRAINING

Riding technique has experienced incredibly rapid development in all disciplines of snowboarding. The following remarks are to be considered as a type of introduction to lead the snowboarder through the complex facets of technique training. The intention is not, however, to describe a single correct technique or resolution, for there is no such thing. These observations and experiences are likewise not to be considered as universal prescriptions; rather, they should be seen as complementing the rider's own ideas and courage to experiment.

Changes in conditioning in snowboarding training also have an effect on riding technique (e.g., poor conditioning hinders riding technique).

Conditioning training should correspond to technique specific demands in snowboarding (e.g., elasticity).

An early start to technique and coordination training is generally important in snowboarding in order to create the best foundation.

Basic Considerations

Technique training contributes to overall athletic performance as an essential factor in snowboarding and to the rider's success. The main task involves acquiring, perfecting, and stabilizing the technical riding skills.

Riding technique is the reflection of the snowboarder. It expresses all types of changes and developments. Therefore, entire areas of athletic ability have a great influence on its manifestation.

Technique training is therefore of great importance in snowboard sports. This is evident, for instance, in the course of the preparation period, in the other types of training (e.g., speed training) that are not done in isolation but in conjunction with technique training.

That's the only way technique training can be made to correspond to the complex demands of snowboarding.

Conditioning and Technique

At every level of the snowboarder's athletic ability the performance factors of conditioning and technique are interrelated. The greatest challenge lies in tuning them in the best way. Often there is an imbalance between these performance factors.

From these connections the following **IMPORTANT POINTS** are derived:

Age and Development

Development of coordination and riding technique for snowboarding can start as early as between six and seven years for children, or later on between twelve and fourteen years for boys and ten to twelve

Coordination can be developed most effectively during childhood.

for girls. These ages are the best for learning coordination.

At this time, training should include general technique practice (see p. 52).

ARGUMENTS AGAINST EARLY SPECIALIZATION are, according to Weineck et al.:

- Lack of reserve in psychological-physical strength potential
- Long-term development requirements
- Excessive ambition on the part of trainers or parents
- Increased dropout rate
- Burnout because of excessive demands

Oftentimes riders don't start snowboarding until after these important development phases. A quality technique training program is particularly important in cases where the best time for developing technique and coordination has been missed.

The Purpose of Technique Training

The goal of technique training in snowboarding consists of developing the best possible coordination of movement. The following components are important, according to Meinel and Schnabl:

Linking Skills

Through linking ability, movements of body parts are effectively coordinated to achieve a movement goal (e.g., active movement of joints used in jumping, as in quick edge changes with simultaneous deep knee bend).

Differentiation Skills

Differentiation skills refer to the degree of fine-tuning of individual movement stages in moving body parts. In top-level riders they are characterized by great precision and economy of movement. As training progresses, they take on increasing importance.

Linking skills in moving various body parts are illustrated here: a deep crouch and attendant angling of the joints used in jumping produce edging on the heel side.

Balancing Skills

These skills enable the body to maintain balance or to recover it through changes in body position, such as in making a safe landing after a jump.

Orientation Skills

Here changes in body position and movement through space and time are controlled by the rider (as in movement changes between two gates in a course).

Rhythmizing Skills

Rhythmizing skills make it possible to grasp a specific rhythm, as in the case of a tight, vertical course, reproduce it, and apply it, as in riding a tight course.

Balancing skills are especially important in achieving a stable position (bending the legs) during the flight phase of a jump.

Reaction Skills

These skills refer to quick application and execution of effective, rapid actions upon a signal. This is a question of reacting with appropriate speed at the most effective moment.

Adjustment Skills

Based on situational requirements, adjustment skills allow changes in the course of movement or substitution of a different movement. That can happen when the radius between gates can no longer be ridden precisely with the waisting radius of the board and the rider is outside of the line. When the normal body position is changed and the body weight is shifted increasingly to the tail of the board, the board can still be edged at the tail in a timely manner.

Movement coordination is developed by means of experience, conception, and the movement program developed by the rider. Because of snowboarding's fast development, this involves continuous learning (acquisition), perfection (improvement), and stabilization (automating) riding skills through repeated and conscious implementation. The goal is application of riding technique to any situation that may arise.

The desired movements should also correspond to the individual rider's circumstances. Situations that are too demanding should be avoided in any case, as they may undermine motivation.

Learning Phases in Technique Training

The process of learning technique is accomplished in several phases. Riding is central to each phase (see Table 5, p. 52). It should be complemented in every phase by additional supporting measures, which are of great importance because of frequent changes in riding technique.

Rhythmizing and orientation skills are evident in running a tight slalom.

Steering with the tail is often the last chance to ride a course well at high speeds; movements must be modified very quickly (adjustment skills).

Connecting and Understanding Phase

The goal of the beginner or the advanced rider in acquiring new techniques should be to develop a concept of movement. That comes from external information (e.g., trainers and videos) as well as from within (implementing technique). The beginner should begin as soon as possible with the first attempts at on-snow training. Comparison between external and firsthand information makes it possible to develop a concept of movement. As training continues, the refinement of that concept is a major goal. The information gleaned from external sources must always correspond to the rider's present level of perception and understanding of movement (e.g., orally).

Gross Coordination Phase

At the end of this phase the rider possesses the major features of how the movements are performed. Simple instruction is usually conveyed orally. Moves are characterized by

- Incorrect applications of strength
- Interruptions
- Jerky movements
- Wrong tempo
- Insufficient range of motion
- Inadequate precision of movement

Retention or learning as a function of how it's is conducted, according to Weineck.

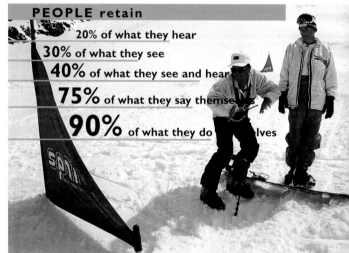

PEOPLE retain

20% of what they hear
30% of what they see
40% of what they see and hear
75% of what they say themselves
90% of what they do themselves

Fine Coordination Phase

At the end of this phase we encounter fine coordination of riding technique. Verbal instructions are elaborated more effectively and the movement concept is refined. This phase is distinguished by the following points:

- Adequate strength expenditure
- Effective rhythm and range of movement
- Pronounced fluidity of movement

Consolidation and Perfection Phase

In this phase riders develop their finest coordination (see Table 5), which they can apply confidently and successfully in unaccustomed and difficult conditions.

Because movements have become automatic, riders now can concentrate on critical points within the overall movements. The following factors of movement are typical of this phase:

- Precision
- Consistency
- Harmony

Table 5. Interrelationships among training factors and neurophysiological aspects of the learning phase, according to WEINECK

Learning phases in development of athletic technique	Training method criteria in technique training	Neurophysiological process of learning motor skills
1. ADJUSTMENT PHASE: The learner adjusts to target exercise.	Formulate first ideas about performing movements, meet requirements through preliminary exercises and basic skills.	Optical, acoustic, verbal, and kinesthetic perceptions produce first areas of interest, intellectual grasp of movements, and pattern change.
2. GROSS COORDINATION PHASE: Movement contains first integrated basic structures.	Movements become integrated, but under restricted conditions, without refining characteristics of individual phases and partial movements. Goal of this phase is integrated basic pattern of how movements are performed.	"Irradiation and stimulation process" = broadening and ascendancy of motivation over inhibition in the brain cortex. The result is an uneconomical and excessive innervation of affected muscles.
3. FINE COORDINATION: The individual phases get their kinetic and dynamic structure; later the entire movement becomes more conscious.	Integrated rough framework is retained. Individual phases and "joint locations" of technique are isolated and practiced individually. Example is now the ideal type of technique. Learning conditions become fairly standardized. Fine development depends on clarifying goals and learning process; fine development = conscious practice.	In the "Concentration Phase" the inhibiting and stimulating processes concentrate on effective innervation of centers and organs. But the whole system of inhibition and stimulation is still quite weak and is susceptible to disruptions. Movements are carried out through sensory, most frequently, optical controls.
4. CONSOLIDATION AND STABILIZATION PHASE: Reaction system is strengthened, i.e., reactions and adaptation respond to external influences and maintain a stable structure.	Consistent performance is achieved through practice under changing conditions and competition conditions. Good reaction and adjustment are the goal. Training for heightened sensitivity to, and awareness of, movement is still important.	Stimulation and inhibition processes become automatic so that movements are accomplished without conscious attention. Innervation patterns become locked into brain cortex. Coordination becomes stable so that attention can be directed to other environmental factors.

General Technique Training

All-around development is important in technique training. It should take place year-round and be integrated into the rest of the training process. General technique training leads to broadening a snowboarder's movement spectrum. It can be developed through many individual sports like inline skating, trampoline, rock climbing, and mountain biking. Additionally, agility courses are recommended for improving balance and coordination.

Going down a trail or riding in deep snow are also part of general technique training.

An essential part of this training, aside from improving basic technique, is its motivating and regenerating quality. That's why Freeriding on the trail should always be part of race training. That avoids stagnation, provides motivation, and leads to active recovery during training. Ball games after training also have a motivating and active regenerative effect in addition to their general coordination benefits.

Special Technique Training

Special technique training focuses on skills needed for racing. It builds on movements learned in general technique training. At its center is development of a specially tailored repertory of techniques appropriate to applicable disciplines. The learning process focuses on acquiring and perfecting integrated movements appropriate to the demands of racing. Individual objectives are subject to the rider's proficiency. This is demonstrated especially in the choice of training methods, contents, and means. Generally in special technique training the important principles of learning movement should be observed at every step

- From the known to the unknown
- From the easy to the difficult
- From the simple to the complex

The systematic approach to special technique training can be divided into the following five stages, according to Schnabl:

- Practice under simplified conditions
- Practice under normal conditions
- Practice under modified conditions
- Practice under difficult conditions
- Practice under competition conditions

Freeriding can complement training; during and after a competition it is relaxing, and should therefore be part of every workout.

In addition to these general observations on systematic training there are several important **BASIC METHODS** that are of particular importance to snowboarders:

A well-developed basic technique (mastery of the turns) makes it easier to learn other skills Snowboarders should be in a physically and psychologically rested condition at the start of training. An exception is technique training after prestressing (see Systematic Support for Training).

- Every training session, even for technique work, begins with a warm-up.
- Technique training should correspond to the individual's existing technique and conditioning.
- In no case should anxiety figure into technique training (e.g., danger of excessive demands and risk of injury).
- Concentration on technical performance should include ample time and composure.
- Board construction should match the individual's existing conditioning and riding skills.
- Freeriding should be part of warm-up as well as technique training.
- Instructions should match the rider's level of accomplishment (content and quantity of information).
- The technique learning process should proceed without long interruptions between workouts; otherwise the effectiveness of the training is reduced.
- A snowboarder's technical skills are subject to psychological and physical fluctuations within meso- and microcycles.

gates, timing edge changes, rhythm of movement, etc.). For development of a preliminary concept of movement, training should be characterized by

- Simplified conditions, i.e., by means of best conditions determined on an individual basis (see Systematic Support for Training)
- Individually tailored instructions on movement (in appropriate amounts) and demonstrations by instructor or friends
- Consistent conditions

As training progresses the beginner has adequate gross coordination to do the movements (see Table 5, p. 52). Grasping the time-space movement structure precedes grasping the dynamic. Often superfluous moves are mixed in with turning motions. But at this point they are pretty much ignored.

It's much more important to emphasize issues such as initiation and control of turns (see Systematic Support for Training). The simplified conditions should be introduced and varied slightly only after a perceptible strengthening of these movement segments in the course of further training. If riders hit plateaus, conditions should be simplified further.

Special Technique Training for Beginners

Training for beginners presupposes ample technique practice on the slopes. Complete turns should be possible on the trail. Beginning training improves general riding technique and can help even those riders who are not interested in racing.

In this training, snowboarders are confronted with riding a set course. They have only a vague idea of the time-space and dynamic movement structure (taking

Training Goals and Content for Beginners

- Develop a concept of motion
- Acquire time-space movement structure
- Acquire dynamic movement structure
- Practice under simplified conditions

Specialized Technique Training for Advanced Racers

Specialized technique training emphasizes refinement of one's conception of movement and the elimination of unnecessary motions, including keeping the upper body quiet with no rotation. Simplified conditions are further reduced. When movements are carried out consistently, the first variations of the normal training conditions can be introduced. Judging adequate consistency is often difficult. The rider or coach should experiment carefully with the variations and complications to conditions. It must be considered if the performance is acceptable (especially for first attempts), or if major impediments to performance are present. If performance problems are observed, training conditions should be appropriately simplified.

The following measures are appropriate **VARIATIONS AND COMPLICATIONS:**

- Training on slopes of different pitch (up to medium steepness)
- Training on different course conditions (limited)
- Variations in distances between gates
- Variations in change of direction (rhythmic and sharply angled)
- Variations in length of course

After further consolidation the technique can be tested in competition. That may often lead to significant technical errors and to backsliding into defects previously eliminated.

Competition becomes an increasingly important part of the overall training process as performance stabilizes. Variations in training conditions and frequent competition build motivation and avoid boredom in training. This step should nevertheless be considered carefully, for jumping into competition too early often leads to reinforcement of mistakes. In addition, the rider should direct increased attention to weaknesses in individual movements such as unweighting the board.

Refinement of movement is closely related to improving anticipation. It should be trained consciously from this point on. Closely connected to it is an increasing perception of distinct movement. Every run should be analyzed verbally with friends or with the coach. This leads to important internal commands that riders can use to improve their performance. That's helpful in deliberate movement, and it often produces an acceleration in the learning process. Especially at dynamic high points in individual turns, internal commands can contribute decisively to setting the right tempo.

In conjunction with verbal analysis, snowboarders should develop their knowledge of riding technique and their powers of observation relative to their own technique and that of other riders by means of videotape or by someone else's observation. Objective evaluation such as videotaping should be used more frequently in training.

Videos are important controls in objective evaluation of performance; they also aid in improving the rider's conception and perception of movement.

In general, snowboarders should begin to discover their individual potential. The way to fine motor coordination involves lots of training and repetitions of movements combined with concentration and deliberation. Training motivation can be furthered by setting intermediate goals (see Periodic and Cyclic Training).

In the foregoing section we have shown that refinement of technique at advanced levels involves, among other things, a progression from the simple to the complex by introducing one element of difficulty at a time. If the new complexity produces a relapse, conditions are simplified once again. Riders who successfully master increasing levels of challenge, and who excel at evaluating their performance, will be able to transfer their new skills from training to competition.

Training Goals and Elements for Advanced Riders:

Refinement of concept of movement

Elimination of superfluous movement

Improvement of component movements

Refinement of control and more precise regulation of movement

Conscious anticipation

Verbal analysis and use of internal commands

Use of objective means of evaluation such as videotaping

Broadening of understanding of riding technique

Testing of technique in competition

Special Technique Training for Top-level Racers

The main training goal at this high level is characterized by two essential components:

Optimum availability of riding technique potential
Resistance to distractions in high-stress situations, such as difficult and important competitions

This training goal is reached by very few riders and only over the course of many years; it's also a never-ending process.

It can be accomplished only through continuous training. The exceptional skills of these riders are manifested through experiments with, and discoveries of, new board materials, new board shapes, and new riding techniques or variations that may lead to success.

This development can also work the opposite way, where the riding technique of top athletes leads to new board technology. In this case even these top-level riders cling to methods and measures used by beginners. This phase is passed through very quickly, however, and the new movement is mastered so completely that it can be successfully applied in competition. The way to a high-level riding technique takes a long time and should therefore be carefully thought out. The degree of technical mastery therefore depends on persistence in dealing with

■ Modifications in psychological state, as in cases of "prestart jitters" or emotional lows
■ Various forms of fatigue (e.g., muscular or emotional)
■ External changes such as weather
■ External pressure to perform, such as directly from opponent in Duel Slalom

Riders at this level can free up their attention from most aspects of movement performance and concentrate entirely **ON THE FOLLOWING POINTS:**

■ Timing anticipation during a run
■ Tactical moves such as keeping Duel Slalom opponent in field of vision
■ Complete utilization of conditioning skills

Timing and anticipation of difficulties are important skills for top-level racers.

Management and control of riding technique takes place without undermining concentration. Moves are done automatically.

Another important point in development of riding technique that affects snowboarders involves finding their best individual and current moves, that is, their riding style. There will never be just one correct way to ride. Generalizations about successful riding styles are therefore impossible to make (see Riding Style and Technique). Every advanced rider advances by experimentation and discovery of the best individual moves for the highest possible performance level. So there can only be measures and methods to help riders realize their potential.

These observations produce **ADDITIONAL IMPORTANT FUNDAMENTALS** for special training for advanced riders:

Adjustment of riding style to changing conditions is aided by practicing under competition conditions and by frequent races.
Further advancement in riding technique is accomplished by experimenting with moves. Possible alternative moves are gone through in the mind and on the course.
Training under greater exertion and at high cadence is absolutely essential for advanced riders who want stability in their moves.

Resistance to fatigue and accompanying conditioning skills will play an ever-increasing role in riding technique for snowboard racing.

This advancement of technique training at the top performance level makes the entire training structure very complex. The relationships to other athletic performance factors now become very clear to the snowboarder, and therefore require direct integration of these factors into technique training. That manifests itself in the systematic measures in training under difficult conditions (see p. 59ff.). These measures are accompanied by objective evaluations such as videotaping or recording times. Verbal analysis is now very precise and deliberate. It is characterized by evaluation by both the rider and the coach.

Physical training is closely connected to an increasingly important component—the rider's psychology. Psychological preparation takes place unbeknownst to many riders. A rider's susceptibility to psychological stress depends on

Frequency of stresses to which the rider is exposed
Mastery of psychological self-control
Knowledge of strengths and weaknesses in skills

A high technical proficiency is therefore obtainable only through frequent, deliberate training under difficult and stressful conditions. Self-control is an important training goal in all of this.

Systematic Support for Training

The following systematic steps help support special training. They depend on the current development of the rider and can be divided into two main categories. The first category refers to training and practicing under simplified conditions. The second category structures training under more difficult conditions.

Special technique training under simplified conditions is applied primarily to beginners, but in the case of advanced or top-level riders it can also be used to get through periods of stagnation, or after layoffs due to injury. In this category belong

- Terrain aids
- Use of equipment
- Shortening of course (even down to one gate)
- Slowed-down performance of moves (e.g., through course setting)
- Orientation aids
- Strengthening of feedback

Terrain Aids

In many ways the terrain influences riding technique. The pitch of the slope and its lateral profile are factors in simplifying training conditions.

For training beginning racers the choice is flat to medium slopes. Speed can be kept low, thereby permitting slower moves. Anxiety level is considerably reduced.

Often riders have problems turning around a gate in one direction. In this case, slopes that tip to the problem side aid the turn and make it easier. The hill should slope in the direction of the desired turn.

The shape of the terrain makes it easier to tip the board and helps with the timing that makes possible a quick and easy direction change. The terrain helps

A course that slopes to the side can help with moves; in this example, the rider finds it easier to cant the board toward the backside in front of the blue gate.

with training and support of weighting and unweighting the board in turns, and it improves sensory motor skills. Choosing flat terrain helps in learning how to perform the moves and rhythm changes. Additionally, it helps advanced and top-level riders improve their cadence and learn the active canting movement in the ankles. For that, gates are very narrow and set in the fall line. Corresponding training on steep terrain is not appropriate, since speed becomes too great.

Getting the rhythm and increasing the tempo can be improved in tight courses on flat slopes.

Use of Equipment

Simplification with equipment can be accomplished by using short poles or cones. They reduce contact points with the body and help diminish anxiety level. They are used especially in rhythm training, since they are so short that they don't interfere with the rhythm.

The right board choice with a view toward the rider's physical capabilities should be explained at this point.

Shortening the Course

The length of the course can create excessive demands on the rider. It should be geared to the rider's conditioning. A beginner's conditioning should not become a limiting factor in race-specific technique training. Consequently, the course should be shortened to suit the individual.

Even at other levels of proficiency the course length should not approach the upper limits of the rider's conditioning. Deterioration in technique must absolutely be avoided.

Slowed-down Performance of Moves

Performing moves at slower speeds can be an important learning aid (see Terrain Aids). At slower speeds over flat terrain, snowboarders can concentrate on running gates. Depending on the discipline, the distance between gates and their offset from the fall line in an angular course help control speed and tempo.

Setting the gates farther apart on flat terrain can reduce the slalom tempo. In Giant Slalom, gates can be set closet together to reduce speed.

Orientation Aids

Orientation aids are often an important aid in technique training. With beginners the orientation problems often consist of choosing the best line through a course. This problem also occurs when advanced and top-level riders experience plateaus; it usually takes the form of timing problems in edge changes.

Orientation aids can be given with markers (e.g., short poles) or with audible signals such as shouts. Audible signals can help a lot with creating a rhythmic movement, and they can be internalized well.

Strengthening Feedback

Snowboarders can improve feedback with the terrain aids already mentioned. Changing edges on a course that tips in the direction of a turn requires a definite change in weighting and unweighting the board; the rider's responsiveness and sense perceptions register that change. The same is true for riding on certain ground shapes.

It should be considered that too much time spent training under simplified conditions can lead to faulty coordination that may become ingrained. Then the moves can't be done under normal conditions.

As a result, simplified conditions work best when used in the **PROPER AMOUNT.**

Excessive simplifications produce a different technique which later on will not meet the demands of competition.

The second category of steps pertains to **SPECIAL TECHNIQUE TRAINING UNDER DIFFICULT CONDITIONS**. These measures are aimed at, and intended to, aid advanced and top-level riders. They are based on the principle of variation, and they facilitate refinement, consolidation, and perfection of race-specific riding technique. With this type of training, the power of motivation must be kept in mind. Here too the fundamental of optimum dosage applies.

The following measures are useful in the second category:

- Changes in external conditions
- Variations in executing moves
- Combining of skills in performing moves
- Practice under time pressure
- Variations in information intake
- Practice after prestressing

Changes in External Conditions

External conditions and their changes are often a performance-limiting factor in races. Riders who do not subject themselves adequately to these conditions in training often experience problems in competition. So training in bad weather conditions can serve as a motivator. In addition, this contributes to flexibility in the rider and in the entire training program. Changes in external conditions are closely linked to variation in information intake (see p. 61).

The following external conditions should be included in training by means tailored to suit the individual:

- Training on different trail conditions
- Choosing steep training slopes
- Lengthening the course
- Choice of slope with blind turns and reduced visibility
- Training in different and very poor visibility (training in poor visibility must be acceptable to the rider because of the increased danger of taking a fall; for less accomplished riders this involves training on mild terrain at lower speeds)

The more variety riders and trainers build into the training program the more versatile the competitors will be; unfamiliar or changing course conditions will not be a major limiting factor in their performance.

Elsewhere we have mentioned how essential it is for competitive snowboarders to be physically flexible. This section points out the importance of being supple and adaptable in other ways. That is accomplished through extensive experience, and by consciously training as many different types of external conditions as possible so that on race day the course will hold no surprises.

Variations in Performing Moves

Choosing slopes of different pitch and variation in setting the course influences variations in breadth of the moves, turn direction, tempo, and use of energy in performing the moves (e.g., unweighting/stretching the legs). When riders build up an extensive repertoire of moves and different ways of performing them, they are better prepared to negotiate any challenges a competition course may present. Extensive practice using such variations and adapting them to external conditions will help riders make choices instantaneously and instinctively. Sufficient training should make such variations second nature to competitors.

Combining Skills in Performing Moves

Combining skills refines and optimizes timing of fast moves. That increases the complexity of the moves because their component parts are performed almost simultaneously. An example is unweighting by means of mild leg extension with simultaneous stretching movement in the ankles to change edges.

Variations in riding a course with a trough: Riders who normally take a direct line (a) should take the wider line (b) inside the trough and use it to vary their moves. Riding a direct line inevitably leads to missing the next gate or to a fall, since the right line based on the trough can't be maintained (see arrows).

Practicing under Time Pressure

Riding for time is essential to preparation for competition. Because of the resulting stress, that has a major psychological and physical effect on many riders and can restrict their performance. Repeated timed runs reduce stress as the rider becomes more accustomed to it. A rider's technique potential is no longer blocked and can again be used to good advantage. Furthermore, time trials develop concentration and are an important measure of the training's effectiveness (see Standard Values).

Time pressure can also play an important role in combining training for technique and conditioning with respect to intervals and repeats (see Training and Prestressing).

Variations of Information Intake

The way information is taken in depends greatly on variations in exterior conditions. For example, information intake can vary in sunny and shady portions of a run. Visual perception is reduced, and compensation is provided by improvement in orientation and balancing skills. Training in poor visibility reduces information intake even more and further encourages use of those two skills.

Practice after Prestressing

Practice after prestressing, or practice in combination with stresses on conditioning, is not inconsistent with the rested state at the start of technique training mentioned earlier. The fundamental requirements for using this training measure are, however, an appropriate amount of special technical skills and a general psychological and physical resilience on the part of the rider. In any case, quality in performing the moves must be preserved.

Additionally, it should be noted that technique training itself leads to high demands, especially given loss of concentration and fatigue of the central nervous system.

The following should be practiced after prestressing:

- Shortening breaks between runs
- Increasing the number of repetitions
- Lengthening of training unannounced
- Including additional tasks in workouts without advance notice
- Lengthening course

Riding Style and Technique

As snowboarding has developed, different riding styles have arisen and have proven successful. This fact proves once again the individuality of snowboarding. A "right" or "wrong" does not exist in this sport. Courage to experiment and discover individual possibilities should be an important training goal of every snowboarder.

Consequently, it's impossible to give universally applicable recommendations. This section should be regarded primarily as a guideline with some important fundamentals on the subject of technique training.

It should facilitate developing an individual's best riding technique and style, and aid the rider by supporting them. Snowboarders must realize that this way is the basis for several disciplines and their further development.

RIDING STYLE AND TECHNIQUE are influenced by the following:

- General continuity of turning technique
- Board, boot, and binding technology
- How and where the equipment will be used
- Individual characteristics of the rider

The four factors are closely related and influence one another. Before snowboarders begin systematic technique training, they should be familiar with the most important interconnections among these four factors and include them in their further planning. Now we're at the point where we can consider putting some of the disparate elements together into more complex moves and developing turning techniques. This will involve weighting, unweighting, edge changes, and controlling turns.

1

How to perform the moves involved in a toeside turn in Giant Slalom.

1: Unweighting and start of turn

2 and **3:** Controlling the turn

4: Unweighting and start of turn

Attentiveness in technique training is focused primarily on weighting, unweighting, and controlling the turn.

In both phases the object is to produce dynamic moves. By means of a controlled vertical movement in the knees and ankles (up-unweighting and down-unweighting), faster unweighting is possible along with a corresponding quick edge change.

In reference to vertical movement, it should be noted that up-unweighting cannot be done with the same speed as down-unweighting because of the preparation step before the actual unweighting occurs.

On the other hand, down-unweighting—quickly moving the body downward—produces unweighting

General Continuity of Turning Technique

General continuity of turning technique refers to how the moves are carried out with reference to timing and function, and to the asymmetrical movements on the board. The following are decisive factors in a structural view of how to perform the moves:

■ Initiating the swing
■ Controlling the turn
■ Weighting and unweighting
■ Timing of these three factors
■ Making asymmetrical moves (toeside, heelside)

Initiating the turn in racing requires that the upper body stay aligned over the center of gravity, mainly the legs and the hips. Newly developed, smaller boards with pronounced waists make it easier to start the turn, and they make it unnecessary to push the body in the direction of the turn, as was formerly necessary. A quiet upper body is important for an overall smooth ride on the smaller boards.

as soon as the move is begun. Down-unweighting therefore makes use of the body's moment of inertia. This produces a new dynamic pressure on the edge as the body checks its downward motion.

In up-unweighting the principle of action and reaction comes into play. The aforementioned preparation step that takes the form of stretching the legs constitutes a weighting applied at the start of the move. The actual unweighting takes place at the end of the stretch movement, followed by renewed weighting through application of pressure in downward movement. The extent of these actions depends on terrain and discipline. In slalom, the moves usually are greatly reduced because of the extremely short time for edge changes. Ideally, the legs drift rhythmically from one side to the other (heelside to toeside) under the upper body. The moves are produced largely by the ankles and resilience in the lower legs.

In giant slalom or in sweeping turns, the rider usually has more time for changing direction. Vertical moves are produced in the ankles and knees. In extremely quick direction changes or in steep terrain, the moves become shorter even in Giant Slalom. In such instances, the impulse for the unweighting movement is produced directly from the ankles, as in slalom.

Consequently the **QUALITY OF THE CANTING MOVEMENT** is of great importance in changing edges. It is dependent on the following:
- Position of the pelvis
- Movement in the ankles
- Timing between vertical movement and the motion of the ankles
- Width of the board

Because of the dynamics of movement and the new board technology, it is possible to maintain a greater degree of canting and higher speed through the turn.

Riders cannot manage today's higher speeds and accompanying centrifugal force in the curves merely by leaning hard into the turns. It's better to avoid leaning into the turns too dramatically because that increases the danger of falling and slows down edge changes; existing exterior forces should be controlled through the rider's muscular strength and direction of the turn.

Moves effective in controlling the turn include the following:
- Dynamic extension or bending of the legs
- Straightening or inclining the body
- Lifting the arms

Different moves of two riders in a tight slalom: The legs of both riders drift almost cyclically back and forth under the upper body. But there is an important difference that should be noted in the moves. Whereas Martin Freinademetz (left) uses legs and hips exclusively to initiate the swings, Dieter Happ (right) uses a pronounced diagonal and vertical movement of the body.

The nature of the turns affects weighting and unweighting of the board (see Fig. 12). There are so-called open and closed turns. With closed turns, the turn begins on a horizontal plane and leads through the fall line right back into the horizontal in a half-moon shape. This involves

- Longer unweighting, weighting, and steering phases
- A greater weighting even in the steering phase because of the force of the curves

With open turns the swings are closer to the fall line. This involves

- A shortening of the unweighting, weighting, and steering phases
- Minimal weighting even in the steering phase.

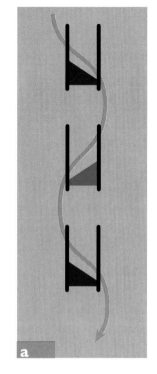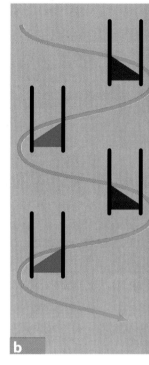

Fig. 12: Open (a) and closed (b) turns.

Clearly, successful snowboarding competitors will need to accumulate experience with both types of turns. They should be addressed thoroughly in training and mastered to the extent possible before tackling them under race conditions.

Another essential point in snowboarding moves is the asymmetrical movement in executing the swing. The oblique stance on the board necessitates different movements and provides

Lifting the arms can help with executing a turn.

TWO DISTINCT MODELS FOR

BASIC MOVES on toe- and heelside. They are characterized in both cases by different

- Mobility in the spinal column, hip, knee, and ankle joints
- Coordination
- Strength development
- Leverage considerations and anthropometry

The asymmetrical stance can be almost identical with top-level riders. Here we see the similarity between Martin Freinademetz and Dieter Krassnig at the same gate in a Giant Slalom. Both riders use different stances (regular and goofy), but there is practically no perceptible difference in the upper body position.

Board Technology

Board technology has recently reached a very high and complex level. As a result, we can only point to some of the essential features here. They are of great importance in riding technique and training. With today's developments, riders can match equipment precisely to their individual requirements and skills.

Board technology means that riders have several determining factors to consider:

- Type of physique (weight, body size, shoe size)
- Riding skills
- Conditioning
- Usage

Since these factors vary greatly among individuals, there is no universal prescription for choosing the right board material. So in the following we'll point only to potential changes in riding technique in conjunction with the board material used.

The following parameters in board materials influence riding technique:

- Waisting
- Width of board
- Length of board
- Stiffness/flex of board
- Symmetry/asymmetry

With time some very distinctive profiles have evolved. As snowboards were used more on difficult slopes, the waisting became more pronounced. Waisting is important primarily for curve radius, optimum edge pressure, and dynamic riding technique. It can be tailored precisely to the rider's needs.

Concerning alpine riding technique, in the past three or four years there have emerged two groups of boards distinguished by their width. The differences are defined as follows:

- Wide boards (up to about 9 inches/ 220 millimeters waist width) and
- Narrow boards (up to 6 1/4 inches/ 160 millimeters waist width)

Riding technique for these two groups is different. Foot placement determines the direction of movement of the ankles. With narrow boards this is aligned with the direction of the board tip; with wide boards, in the direction of the inside curve. Foot placement depends greatly on foot size and individual build. This means that riders with bigger feet need wider boards so they don't continually drag their heels or toes in the snow. With narrow boards, edge changes can be done more quickly and the board seems to react quicker. With wider boards it's easier to execute the curve radius of turns, and on steeper slopes the rider has better control.

Board width is independent of snowboarding discipline. It's possible for slalom boards to be a little wider than boards for Giant Slalom or Super G. Board length primarily influences speed. Long boards are used for high speeds.

The stiffness or flex of a board is keyed mainly to the rider's individual physique, such as body weight and size. Conditioning should also be considered.

Stiffer boards are more stable in a curve; accordingly, they must be ridden more actively, and that is possible only to a certain extent in the case of lightweight riders. Lower body weight produces too little edge pressure. A softer board will give these riders the optimum edge pressure. The use of asymmetrical or symmetrical boards depends primarily on how they will be used.

Asymmetrical boards will still be available as long as slalom continues to exist. They are suited to courses with tight curves and are easier to correct in tough courses. Symmetry predominates in Giant Slalom and Super G and is also used by riders in Duel Slalom.

	Symmetrical Construction	Asymmetrical Construction
Slalom	35%	65%
Giant Slalom	100%	0%
Super G	100%	0%

Usage of symmetrical and asymmetrical boards according to discipline

- Distance between gates (size of turn radius)
- Degree of direction change (as with widely offset gates)
- Pitch of slope
- Trail conditions (e.g., firm or icy)
- Speed

Usage

Usage determines the demands the board will be subjected to and the choice of the best board. In racing the demands are defined by the individual disciplines. Those demands are characterized by the following factors:

Individual Traits

Individual traits constitute a large part of athletic ability. They have already been addressed thoroughly (see p. 12). Individual traits are also important in selecting board material. They are crucial in experimenting with different board technologies and in choosing the board that feels just right. They are subject to continuous development and flexibility in training and are the most important factor in achieving the best riding technique. The most important of these traits are

- Conditioning
- Technique and coordination
- Psychological traits
- Physical traits

Many riders, like Gerry Ring, prefer very narrow boards.

Leg technique is fundamental, but it can vary greatly, as with Nicolas Conte (far left) and Martin Freinademetz (left). Both techniques work.

Different body positions on the heelside at the same gate with Dieter Happ (above) and Gerry Ring (below).

Unweighting: Karlheinz Zangerl (left, above) and Dieter Krassning (left) initiate their moves differently in this Duel Slalom course. Whereas Zangerl uses a nearly upright position for unweighting, Krassnig demonstrates a very low position.

Plateaus in Riding Technique

In spite of technical training riders can get stuck on plateaus. That can happen at any level. These learning plateaus can have various causes and are tough to eliminate. Riders should stick to their training carefully so they can react to any stagnation that may arise. Causes for plateaus can include

- Attempt to learn too much information
- Excessive demands in the face of fatigue
- Lack of information
- Lack of motivation
- Inadequate conditioning
- Neglect of technique training
- Injuries and anxiety

Trying to Learn Too Much Information

In so-called senso-motor regression the rider's moves stagnate as the result of intensive technique training in combination with a simultaneous external overload of verbal information. In this instance, the rider should take breaks to process information, and take in less verbal instruction.

Excessive Demands in the Face of Fatigue

Intensive technique training is often closely connected to muscle fatigue, and that usually produces general fatigue.

Fatigue is a protective mechanism that the body uses against excessive demands, and it's a clear signal to take a break from training. Riders should therefore get to know their bodies better as training progresses so that they can react quickly to the signs of fatigue mentioned in the next section. Continuing technique training in such a condition often detracts from technique.

Characteristic signs of muscular fatigue, according to Hettinger:

- **Deterioration of skills**
- **Keeping up any given performance by using performance reserves**
- **Slow and uncertain motor activity and attendant impaired coordination**
- **Slowing down of reaction time**
- **Loss of motivation**

Falls often lead to injuries that can have a major psychological effect on the rider.

Lack of Information

Progress in riding technique can also be retarded if the rider doesn't have a clear concept of how to execute the moves. This often happens because movements already done are interpreted incorrectly. A lack of information is often at the root of this problem. Concepts of how moves should be performed interfere with corrections and can't be put into practice.

Learning plateaus can last a long time because the movement pattern may already be automatic. So the disadvantages of the existing concept of movement must be understood. At this point questions such as these arise:

- What do you experience when you perform this move?
- What important points in the move can be mentioned?
- Are there orientation points during the move?
- Are you using internal commands? If so, which ones?

Within this process a relaxed training atmosphere is particularly important, for in stressful situations moves that have already become automatic appear again almost compulsively. At every level of performance the systematic steps for training already mentioned should be used.

Lack of Motivation

The rider's frame of mind and motivation are important factors in technique plateaus. Training that incorporates lots of variety, plus consciousness of one's athletic demands and goals, are basic requirements for good motivation.

Inadequate Conditioning

The increasing importance of conditioning is evident with respect to technique plateaus. Intensive technique training and competitions pose increasing demands on a snowboarder's conditioning. Long-standing lack of conditioning can therefore be the main cause of early muscular and general fatigue. In the long run that leads to stagnation in technique.

Neglect of Technical Training

As riders analyze possible causes of stagnation they should examine their overall technique training. They should avoid technique training that's too narrow in scope or that does not address their personal goals.

Injuries and Anxiety

These factors lead to plateaus, longer layoffs for injuries, and anxiety as a result of bad falls. An injured snowboarder is considered a patient and has to behave as one. Training that starts too early can lead to long-term serious stagnation of the rider's development.

The prescribed rehabilitation time should be adhered to without fail. Thereafter, training in all areas should be slow and should increase at a rate tailored to the individual (see "Training Principles"). Especially in technique training, practice should be intensified under simplified conditions in accordance with performance level. Too much too soon can lead to injuries.

Another type of technique plateau involves anxiety after bad or repeated falls. It's often a long process to get rid of anxiety, and it requires lots of patience on the part of the rider and coach.

The basic requirement for a stable and long-lasting elimination of this problem is a training atmosphere free of tension, stress, and pressure to perform. The affected rider has to adhere more than ever to the basics of technique training (p. 52). Snowboarders who have no coach should pay particular attention to these basics.

But consistent attention to these fundamentals is not enough to do away with anxiety. An example should make this clear: A racer who is successful in national-level competition has no problems with steep courses and icy conditions. The racer is confident and controls the board under all conditions. In a race where the rider has a chance of winning, icy conditions and steep terrain produce a bad fall and the rider is injured. The result is that the rider is no longer free of anxiety when training in steep and icy terrain.

This example demonstrates how a previously neutral stimulus—racing on steep and icy terrain—which before the fall triggered no reactions, can turn into an anxiety-producing stimulus. After that happens a course with those conditions inspires fear.

The entire phenomenon is much like a learning process where emotions, conceptions, or fears are acquired in the face of specific situations.

Methods for resolving this problem involve unlearning or breaking the effect of the stimulus that usually produces anxiety—a steep, icy course in this case.

The basic requirement for eliminating inappropriate reactions is total physical relaxation, for example, through autogenous training. That excludes psychological tension of the type that exists in the presence of fear. A rider who is relaxed cannot simultaneously feel anxiety, and vice versa.

The rider is exposed systematically and gradually in a state of relaxation to the signal that produces anxiety (the icy, steep course). The possibilities in this instance are

```
Establishing fear hierarchy
Devising special relaxation
training (e.g., autogenous or
mental training) before every
workout
Training under simplified
conditions
Verbalizing how the movements are
carried out and how the training
is going
Gradually eliminating simplified
conditions
Temporarily suspending training
plans relative to competition
```

Planning the gradual introduction to the anxiety-producing stimulus is guided by the created fear hierarchy. It provides information on the number and degree (strength, dominance) of the anxiety-producing moments of a stimulus. There are no universal remedies for the previously mentioned possibilities. They must be used and adapted individually according to conditions.

It should not be forgotten that this is a long and time-consuming process in which relapses should be avoided wherever possible.

The use of psychological training such as mental or autogenous training (see Psychological Training) is unexplored territory for most riders. But these types of training can be of great importance in technique training.

Another important measure is inclusion of longer training breaks in the present training process. That provides good variety and can help diminish anxiety.

Competition and Preparation

Competition occupies an increasingly important place in a snowboarder's development. Their training is increasingly organized around the season's important competitions. That's where various training goals and objectives are realized. But competitions can also be like training. So preparation for competition is not accomplished only through training. Development or control competitions should be scheduled into the training process. Comparing performances in racing is a proving ground for snowboarders, where they must apply the performance qualifications they have developed through training. The uniqueness of competition lies in the qualification and final runs, in duel competition (as in Duel Slalom), in the constraints of the rules, the psychological changes before and during the competition, and in the varying external conditions. These produce psycho-vegetative stimuli on the racer that scarcely come up in training.

Competition imposes high demands on the rider's psychological capacities. This is especially evident when riding against an opponent in Duel Slalom.

Fig. 13: Tasks involved in control, according to Weineck.

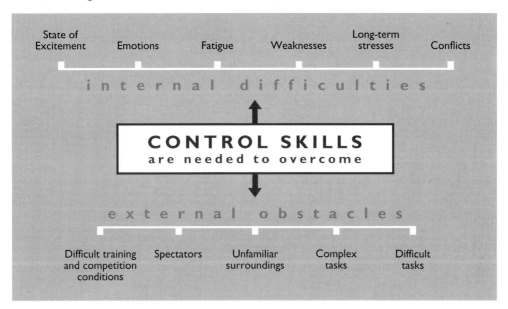

Regulation and management of actions in competition, and their conscious use in reference to competitive goals in snowboarding, require increased psychological preparation. The following possibilities exist in snowboard training:

■ Development of cognitive, motivational, and emotional components of snowboard racing
■ Development of a process of psychological regulation
■ Preparation of behavior programs

In development competitions snowboarders can further their personal skills in accordance with their requirements.

Tactical ability becomes evident in conscious decisions made during the race. It is based primarily on control (see Fig. 13), which is developed in competitionlike situations in training and solidified by application to competition.

Psychological Training

Psychological training is of great importance to snowboard racers for their athletic development, given the increase in competitions (see Complex Athletic Ability). But the following observations are important even for beginners:

Coping with psychological demands is crucial in snowboard training and competition. Warming up immediately before competition is of the utmost importance. Top-level athletes use preparation rituals that have been developed through experience over time. They usually involve warming up the body, analyzing the imminent task, and special activities such as checking the board once again; these preparations always follow the same familiar pattern.

But often these important rituals are left out, especially by beginners, or are interrupted (see Plateaus after Falls). This frequently leads to a major stagnation in the overall training process.

The following explanations are important parts of the ability to handle psychological stress in snowboarding sports. They demonstrate their importance as valid training goals and should contribute to the further development of existing behaviors that at top levels help riders deal with psychological and physical stresses. The following two **BASIC QUESTIONS** are important in approaching training, according to Eberspacher:

■ What produces psychological stress and what conditions influence it?
■ What methods are useful in controlling psychological stress?

The following three areas of psychology in view of existing **PERSON-ENVIRONMENT-CHANGE-RELATIONSHIP** are important in reference to these questions:

- Perception
- Test behavior
- Instrumental behavior

All three areas are important parts of being able to withstand psychological stress. They are worth cultivating and improving through training.

Optimizing perception occurs, according to Eberspacher, through gathering important information for planning and preparation for stress conditions. There are three important **COMPLEXES OF CONDITIONS FOR PREPARING FOR EXISTING STRESSES:**

- Organizational conditions
- Material conditions
- Personal conditions

Organizational conditions refer to travel, accommodations, prevailing weather, food, scheduling, press conferences, and so forth. Material conditions for which the rider must be prepared are the particular conditions of the training or competition terrain (snow and light conditions, weather, setting of course, etc.) and of the board material (material

Preparations for the start turn into personal rituals.

preparation, shape, etc.). Personal conditions include the rider's individual condition (in training, too), opponents (especially in Duel Slalom), and even the spectators. Appraisal of the anticipated stress situation (competition) is therefore characterized by gathering adequate information in three condition complexes. The content of the information determines how it is evaluated. So, for instance, the rider's psychological state before the start of a race is characterized by changeable and uncertain confidence. This condition should be reduced as much as possible through personal, material, and organizational conditions. Another possibility in psychological stress training is regulation of test behavior. That is based on the effectiveness and management of internal messages in stressful situations. Snowboarders who can, by means of internal dialogue, successfully make themselves confident and ready to perform, are carrying out a fundamental skill in dealing with stressful situations.

The third possibility for psychological training that is often addressed is instrumental behavior and real life training. That develops and optimizes specific behavior patterns that can be retrieved in stressful situations. Emotional processes are a major interference in a racer's behavior pattern (anxiety, nervousness, etc.). Oftentimes they can't be addressed through more training (see Plateaus in Riding Technique). They require use of nonmotor training and techniques that control the rider's psychology.

Basically two different training methods can be used. According to Eberspacher, these are motor training, which has already been addressed (e.g., technique training), and nonmotor training, which we'll have a look at now.

In nonmotor training methods, the emphases lie in processes of speaking, thinking, and conceptualizing. Motor and nonmotor methods are not mutually exclusive in training, but complement each other and often occur simultaneously. Volpert distinguishes between external and internal realization in nonmotor training.

External realization deals with a speech and communication process. Here an exchange takes place, as if between coach and rider in anticipation of an imminent stress. This exchange process is always present in training and preparation for competition. It is not limited to technical corrections, but refers to the entire content of training and competition (tactics, organization, etc.).

Internal realization includes observational and mental training. Observational training encourages seeing and conceptualizing moves. It can take the form of films or photo sequences. Mental training, according to Volpert, involves a systematic, repeated, conscious conceptualization of a skill to be learned without actually performing the skill at that time.

Self-conceptualization can be done in various ways. In subvocal training riders talk themselves through executing a move. In concealed perception training, riders imagine another racer while performing certain moves. The riders imagine the moves repeatedly. Ideomotor training pertains to carrying out a move. Riders perform the move in their imagination. Conceptions of moves that have already been performed are also added in as support. Snowboarders should strive to master ideomotor training. That often involves the first two methods.

The workings of mental training are covered in sports and professional literature. Mental training therefore is **WIDELY APPLICABLE**. It involves

■ Warming up mentally before
  competition
■ Applying technical plateaus
  (see p. 68)
■ Relearning riding technique

There are a couple of important requirements for mental training (especially for ideomotor exercises) that are particularly important in the acquisition phase. The following **HINDRANCES** can have a negative impact on mental and overall training (see Fig. 13, p. 71):

■ Conflict situations (including in
  the social sphere)
■ Pressure to perform
■ Unfamiliar surroundings
■ Lack of motivation
■ Excessive ambition
■ Leaving out steps that comprise
  moves
■ Ineffectual, ill-considered
  changes in performing moves

Hindrances can largely be eliminated from training and competition by acquiring effective relaxation techniques. They are useful because stress and relaxation are mutually exclusive. The most familiar **WAYS TO CONTROL PSYCHOLOGY** are

■ Autogenous training
■ Relaxation-mobilization activity
■ Progressive muscle relaxation
■ Biofeedback
■ Psychotonic training
■ Desensitization procedures
■ Yoga

The methods presented here for improving behavior patterns are useful at any given time only in conjunction with the rider's conviction. Building up that conviction and applying the behavior pattern to goal setting requires flexibility and confidence.

According to Eberspacher the following are five **TRAINING GOALS FOR COPING WITH PSYCHOLOGICAL STRESS:**

■ Developing perception of
  situations
■ Developing management of internal
  dialogues
■ Improving instrumental behavior
  possibilities and requirements
■ Developing relaxation techniques
■ Developing convictions about the
  effectiveness of these points even
  in tough situations

Free
style

Freestyle riders experience fun, creativity, individuality, coordination, speed, concentration, and conditioning all in one. This list is of course only a fragment of what Freestyle really involves. Whether philosophy or trend, the discipline is developing in both ways. It's another important part of snowboarding sports.

In order to understand Freestyle thoroughly, a brief look at how it came about is in order. At first there were Powderboards, lots of idealism, a wealth of ideas, and great fun in experimenting.

External influences played a major part. Surfing and skateboarding already existed. With the discovery of snowboards a new terrain—snow—offered many a chance to develop their moves all year long. Parallels to sports with similar moves existed at first only in the minds of a few stalwarts like Terry Kidwell. At that time, the concepts and ideas of these idealists were way ahead of board technology and riding techniques. Nobody knew exactly where snowboarding was headed. But the premonition of a fascinating sport was already there.

The first tricks didn't have much to do with the fascination with moves inherent in skateboarding and surfing. The new Freestyle was too unattractive, and consequently not much in demand. But the idealists kept experimenting. They recognized the close relationship between board technology and riding technique.

Suddenly the moves became more technically advanced, and an increasingly large audience began to take interest. At this stage of its development riders like Craig Kelly, Burt Lamar, Terry Kidwell, and Shaun Palmer were moving forces in Freestyle. These Freestyle personalities gave rise to such images as the rebel image of Shaun Palmer. These images determine expression and style, and they became increasingly evident in interpreting tricks and hits.

Unmistakable riding styles sprang up. The resulting mixture of play with one's own body, the variety of movement, and the riders' individual styles increasingly captured the spirit of youth.

The further development of Freestyle became essential with improvements in board technology and riding technique. The recognition of the close connection between these two components became a major factor in the sport's development. Even today it defines not only Freestyle, but the entire sport of snowboarding.

With the construction of halfpipes yet another element of skateboarding was captured in snow. Halfpipes offered the opportunity to experiment to the fullest. They made it possible to keep practicing moves. The influences of skateboarding were clearly recognizable in the elements of the moves. Snowboarding Freestyle was strongly influenced by skateboarding. The start of the nineties began another major development thrust for Freestyle.

The great popularity of Freestyle in the nineties was the result of several factors. The most important ones are

- Major improvements in board technology and the resulting possibilities of Freestyle-boards
- Construction of good halfpipes by machines developed specifically for the purpose and the accompanying rapidly increasing level of Freestyle
- Development of appealing competitions

Riders like Craig Kelly built the popularity of Freestyle.

Modern
halfpipes have
clearly raised
performance levels.

Riders like Terje Hakonson
are the embodiment
of talent.

conditions for practice and competition.

The development of appealing disciplines for competition underscores the great interest in Freestyle and its increasing level of technique in performing moves.

In Freestyle, competitions have become a challenge for the riders' physical skills. Freestyle, like no other snowboarding discipline, with its unmistakable character and uniqueness, stands slightly at odds with the concept of athletic performance. But the number of competitions at all levels of performance, the rapidly rising performance level of the riders, and the quest for success appear to be sharply on the increase even in Freestyle. So a certain concept of performance can no longer be avoided.

Grim determination in training and competition could quickly undermine the typical "Freestyle-fun." Determination and tension are, however, surely the worst conditions for retaining the individuality and creativity that are so important in Freestyle.

This discipline, along with the entire sport of snowboarding, now stands before a unique opportunity to eliminate these negative phenomena, which unfortunately crop up all too often in performance sports. That should be self-evident, but it will require a lot of time and patience.

Training surely can provide typical Freestyle fun as well as a certain performance component.

A first attempt to reach this all-important goal for the entire sport should now be made for Freestyle.

If this is not done, organized, high-level competition will fail to draw some of the sport's most talented riders. The challenge of finding the right mix of competition and fun will require the attention of athletes, trainers, race organizers, snowboarding associations, and owners and operators of snowboarding areas. Continued growth of the entire sport depends on the success of this endeavor.

With these developments Freestyle definitively went its own way. This independence signified the start of a new individuality for Freestyle riders. Today hits and tricks spring from the creativity that has spontaneously developed within the discipline.

The variety and degree of difficulty of tricks and hits has greatly increased at top levels of Freestyle in recent years. This is especially clear in riders like Terje Hakonson. Many moves can be executed only with great difficulty because of their complexity. But not only the difficulty of the moves has increased, but also the quality, and that's even more important.

This fact was made possible only by the tremendous advances in board technology already mentioned. Individuality is of supreme importance here. Freestylers can find the optimum board construction for their physical requirements.

Increased performance levels have been hurried along especially by construction of high-quality halfpipes. Great halfpipes can now be built with newly developed machines. Halfpipes offer the best

FREESTYLE AND TRAINING

The clock is ticking for training in Freestyle. For many dyed-in-the-wool freestylers this may not seem inconceivable, but the technical development already mentioned and the riders' generally fast-rising level make the step to consistent training absolutely essential. The first indications of this tendency have been evident for some time at top levels of Freestyle.

If we want to do away with current reservations concerning a new and different training, we should look at how technique has developed up to this point. The methods for learning a trick were based largely on the principles of

- Learning through experience
- Learning through trial and error

The first learning principle has always been important, but the second one can, without doubting Freestylers' daring and willingness to accept risks, lead to some painful experiences. These learning methods also result in frequent plateaus in developing technique. A less painful method has its advantages.

Another important point that calls for systematic training is the time factor. Success comes more quickly and increases motivation to develop further. The concept of training doesn't mean abandoning the freedom that has so far existed in Freestyle practice. In this context training rather involves support and advancement of individuality and creativity. Freestylers first discover their abilities, experiment with them, and refine them in training. Naturally, this path unfolds differently for every rider. That's precisely what constitutes the variety and uniqueness of Freestyle.

It's not easy to recognize your own abilities and use them effectively. Oftentimes people think they're at the upper limits of their ability, even though they haven't yet exhausted their potential. The following observations should provide the basis for developing your abilities and for putting them to best use:

The fascination of Freestyle lies in experimenting with your own abilities.

The Training Concept

Before freestylers begin systematic training they should have a clear understanding of their goals and expectations:

- Do they ride solely for fun and are they happy with their present skills, or do they want to improve their technique significantly and even enter competition?
- How much time is available without neglecting other important things such as school and work?
- Are they prepared to invest more time in training than previously?

The goal of training is improvement in Freestyle performance. The motivations for that can be very different. Performance depends on athletic ability, which is described in detail in the racing chapter (see p. 12).

The existing approach to Freestyle training matches the performance structure of this discipline (see p. 82). The term performance structure denotes the character of the individual stress components (e.g., speed and coordination). Accurate knowledge about the current performance structure of Freestyle is very important to purposeful training, since the discipline is characterized by significant development.

Freestyle training is subject to certain fundamentals (see p. 12). Some of these principles are particularly vital to Freestyle. We'll explain them briefly here and take them up later in the chapter. They include the principles of

- Consciousness
- Concreteness
- Appropriateness
- Individuality and Age-appropriateness

Consciousness

The rider's consciousness of overall training is too frequently underestimated. Before learning how to perform a trick, it's really important to understand specific moves that comprise it (e.g., starting a body rotation by turning the head) and why they're done. If that's neglected, the exercise can become frustrating and undermine motivation.

The freestyler's consciousness is not limited to the technique of moves, but includes all objectives of Freestyle training plus the rider's individual requirements. It should function independently of each freestyler's existing performance level.

Complex moves like this one in Boardercross require deliberate execution.

Concreteness

Concreteness is very important in Freestyle. It is closely connected to movement perception. Oftentimes this principle is enough to make moves clear and conscious to freestylers. Videos of how to perform moves or a slowed-down version of important moves can often help.

In addition, practicing parts of moves contributes to psychomotor understanding of how to do a complex move.

Appropriateness

Appropriateness in training or practice refers to the freestyler's skill level. Training should never place excessive demands on the rider's skill. Otherwise anxiety and injuries may be the result. Progress in training under these conditions is very difficult.

Individuality and Age-appropriateness

These two terms embody an important principle for Freestyle training. They are the most important points in development of this snowboarding discipline.

Freestylers' individuality is demonstrated by their special skills, plus their personal expression in jumps and tricks. Their development is possible only with continual attention to the overall personality of the freestyler. A rider who tries to imitate someone

else's style will make no more progress than one who trains according to a monotonous workout schedule.

Training rich in variety and fun, plus the experimentation with one's own skills already mentioned, makes it possible to achieve individuality.

Age-appropriateness is the most important fundamental from a medical standpoint (see Important Training Tips for Young Freestylers, p. 92). It should be explained more thoroughly here, since it is crucial to year-round fun and continued health.

Freestyle is the snowboarding discipline that most speaks to youth. When you start training for it, you have to be ready for enormous physical strain. Young freestylers need to put the brakes on their ambition. If a young body becomes overtaxed, serious damage to the movement apparatus may be the result. That often means leaving the sport. Freestylers have their bodies and abilities just once and should use them wisely and deliberately.

The following concrete objectives for Freestyle training can be formulated from the preceding observations:

- Development of a varied foundation of conditioning and coordination based on the requirements of Freestyle performance
- Rapid and lasting learning of how to perform moves
- Matching of equipment to the individual's needs
- Finding individual strengths and a distinct style
- Experimentation with how to perform moves
- Refinement of technique and expression
- Development of one's own potential to perform moves

Young snowboarders have just what it takes for Freestyle—but only with age-specific, individual training.

PERFORMANCE IN FREESTYLE

Disciplines

The tremendous development of Freestyle in recent years can be understood according to what's gone on in competition.

Various disciplines have developed based on the freestylers' creativity and imagination. At first they were strongly influenced by skateboarding. Freestyle's rapid development in all areas has made it increasingly autonomous.

One of the most popular and impressive competitions is the halfpipe. It's a major part of the ever-increasing familiarity enjoyed by the overall sport of snowboarding. Just a short a while ago it was prohibitively expensive to construct halfpipes. As a result, only very few winter resorts had a halfpipe and a chance to train for it and for possible competitions. Because of developments in machine technology for constructing halfpipes and for the accompanying expenditures for building and installation, there is no longer a shortage of halfpipes in winter sports areas.

The type of construction of a halfpipe is closely linked to the rider's level of performance. Today's very high halfpipes for top-level freestylers are not suited to beginners because of their excessive demands on technique. Beginners should start out in lower halfpipes if possible. The following criteria of halfpipes affect performance:

- Height of the wall
- Height of the vertical part (verts)
- Radius of the transition
- Pitch of slope in the fall line
- Width of flat part (flats)

Modern machines make it possible to set up perfect halfpipes.

In halfpipe, riders show the judges individually created series tricks and hits. The criteria for judging focus on

- Height and level of difficulty of the jumps
- Variety of tricks
- Harmony of the run
- Style and expression in execution

A specified number of riders qualify for the final runs, and the winner is selected from at least two final runs.

A type of competition that is particularly popular on regional and national levels is the so-called Obstacle Course. In these competitions riders demonstrate tricks and hits in their runs, similar to halfpipe; the course consists of steep walls, jumps, quarter-pipes, and so forth. Runs are evaluated by a panel of judges as in halfpipe.

Another very new but already very popular discipline is Boarder-cross. It is one of the first disciplines that includes elements from racing as well as from Freestyle. As a result, alpine racers and freestylers take part in the competitions.

Boardercross consists of various obstacles that must be jumped over or ridden around. Here the object is to finish in the quickest time. Riders have up to six opponents who all start together and whom they try to beat to the finish line. The runs are set up at the start in such a way that every rider has enough room to negotiate the course. According to the rules, an elimination system is used; the two fastest riders get another round until the final winner is determined.

A special form of competition involves jump or air style contests. These competitions are run primarily at the top levels. They are very spectacular and appealing to the spectators.

Riders in this event demonstrate a specified number of varied jumps from their repertoire as they take off from a big jump. Hits are judged by a panel according to their level of difficulty, height, execution, and the rider's individual expression. The rider with the highest total points is the winner. In the so-called high jump contest, the rider jumps over a bar in the transition of a quarter-pipe or halfpipe. The bar must

not be touched. The height of the bar on the coping is adjustable; after the height has been cleared, it is raised. The rider who makes it over the highest bar is the winner.

Competition disciplines and their rules are still subject to frequent changes. Exact predictions on their further development are not possible in the Freestyle arena. But the disciplines mentioned will thrive in the future and contribute measurably to the growth of the sport. For a better understanding of the dramatically increasing level of performance, it will be useful to take a look at how Freestyle has developed.

Boardercross racing requires technical and tactical skills.

Air style contests, like this one in Innsbruck, Austria, are especially fascinating to spectators.

Development

A look toward the beginnings reveals parallels to racing. Motion experiences and their effectiveness in locomotion existed only in distantly related sports such as surfing. Similarities in movements could be transferred from skateboarding. Conditions changed with the fixed, fundamentally heavier snowboard (in comparison to the skateboard) and with its use on snow. The result was a complete reconstruction of the repertory of moves from the application of skateboarding experiences.

At that time no one had any concept of the sport. Moves were developed by trying various things, and by relatively difficult methods. Eliminating painful falls was a basic requirement and the price for success in Freestyle. Moves were tried without much fore-thought. They were often based on movements from skateboarding.

As moves were refined, the way was opened up for talent. This became a basic element of Freestyle sports and remains so today. The fundamental traits of talent are especially evident in coordination. Several top-level riders dominate today's fields with this talent. It is essential to success, but is not the only ingredient. Talent can unfold and develop only under external development processes such as training under favorable conditions. The skills that make up freestylers' talent can develop from there, but must not. Among extremely successful top-level freestylers these talents seem ever greater, and they seem to develop from the outside. So talent in

Extremely good coordination was evident in Terje Hakonson even in the early competitions.

Freestyle is not merely an inherent quality, but one that is subject to development through training.

These conclusions should provide important motivation for all freestylers with respect to pur-poseful training, which can have a decisive influence on further development in Freestyle.

Examining performance structure yields important information on how to approach training. This approach should continually be updated, based on the rapid development of the sport, and is connected to ongoing scrutiny of the individual performance components. The following observation is based on the model of athletic ability (see p. 12) and applies that model to Freestyle.

This is good news for all aspiring Freestyle riders. For even though inborn talent gives some competitors an initial advantage, intelligent and purposeful training will help most people narrow or eliminate the gap between their performance and that of the more talented freestylers. Particularly at top levels of competition, where results are separated by only the smallest margins, skills development in training will play an increasingly decisive role on competition days.

Physical Performance Factors

The physical performance factors of endurance, strength, speed, and agility are crucial to Freestyle. Together they form the basis for effective and productive technique training. Their development is therefore an important training goal.

Endurance

Freestyle training is characterized by frequent repetitions of moves in series, as in halfpipe or obstacle courses. In competitions the rider has to make it through several runs and still be in good shape for the finals. For these conditions, the rider's general and Freestyle-specific endurance is very important. A complete run in training or competition will be determined by endurance and jumping ability. Runs are characterized by very quick contractions of the muscles employed, for instance, during take-offs. Between jumps, on the flats, there is essentially no recovery. Muscles are working anaerobically (without

Additionally, jumping ability supports moves during their execution, as in quickly pulling up the legs while in the air. The strength potential of a freestyler is evident also in cushioning landings, in a low approach to a jump on the flats, and of course in riding.

Speed and jumping ability are especially evident at takeoff.

Resistance to fatigue and jumping endurance are important fundamentals in halfpipe competitions.

oxygen). Endurance in Freestyle therefore means resistance to fatigue and jumping endurance. Resistance to fatigue has another meaning, though. Physical fatigue is very closely linked to central fatigue (see Excessive Demands in the Face of Fatigue, p. 68). It leads to a deterioration in performing moves. It's a major disadvantage in executing complex moves and can lead to an increased risk of injury.

Adequate training, nutrition, and rest are the key ingredients in avoiding physical and central nervous system fatigue. Endurance underlies the other physical performance factors and contributes to achieving the highest possible levels of strength, speed, and agility.

Strength

Strength is one of the most important performance factors in Freestyle. A certain muscular development is necessary for that, but level of strength should not be equated with muscle mass. Excessive muscle mass also means greater body weight, and that's not advantageous in Freestyle. The determining strength component is jumping ability. Its quality is evident in nearly all applications, but especially at takeoff. Intensity at takeoff is clear in the case of riders like Hakonson because of the height of their hits.

That intensity is achieved by a rapid straightening of the legs and ankles. These explosive moves are possible only through special training of the applicable muscle groups and existing talent. In this respect, riders with lots of quick, white muscle fibers (see p. 24) have an advantage.

Speed

Speed is very important in practically all moves in Freestyle. It is closely linked to jumping ability and often has a major effect on the way in which moves are performed. Many spin tricks are possible only at extremely high speeds. Speed in executing moves is supported by well-developed reaction speed. It is extremely important in Freestyle for timing and move corrections.

Quickness is best developed during one's youth. Young freestylers consequently stand before a unique opportunity to develop and enrich these skills and use them to their greatest potential.

Agility

The importance of agility in Freestyle is the result of its exceptional variety and complexity of moves. The way to becoming a fine freestyler therefore involves very good mobility in the entire movement mechanism. The current forms of takeoff, rotation, stretching, and down moves are often attainable only by means of this agility. Also the flow of movement, its harmony and expression are dependent on this

of technique in the last few years. Hits and tricks can be divided essentially into two categories: one with ground contact (takeoff, holding, and support phases and landing), and the other without ground contact (flight phases) (see p. 99). In both instances critical developments have been carried out. These should be regarded as outgrowths of today's advanced board technology and of the construction of improved halfpipes.

The following are noteworthy developments in takeoffs:

- Fundamentally greater takeoff strength because of enhanced jumping ability
- Much improved timing on takeoff
- Improved intra- and intermuscular coordination (effective succession of muscle contractions)

The following are consequences for flight stages:

- Longer flight, with much greater height in flight phases
- Much greater expression resulting from longer flight
- Increased number of turns
- Heightened dynamic of movement
- Optimal possibilities of movement around all three body axes
- Simultaneous or sequential turns around several body axes

From these findings on technique development, the value of the following becomes clear:

- The best possible takeoff
- Improved conditions for expressiveness
- General increase in complexity of moves

Overall riding technique has improved because of fundamentally improved board technology and through maximizing and refining the execution of tricks and hits.

The following considerations are particularly important for Freestyle with respect to the components of coordination. The components are closely connected to one another, and they influence each other.

Expression and harmony of movement are best supported by good agility.

important performance factor. Muscles that cannot extend completely reduce strength development, and consequently the quality of takeoffs.

Agility is of compelling importance in development of technique and coordination. In the future it will become increasingly important with respect to a rider's expressiveness. A further reason for agility training involves avoidance of injury. The physical demands make this absolutely necessary.

Technique and Coordination

As already explained, the most important performance factors are technique and coordination. In all of snowboarding, Freestyle surely places the highest demands on these skills. The high demands become evident when you look at the development

Linking

The best linking of movements in body parts such as the head and torso is an essential component of Freestyle. It permits harmonious moves and is responsible for the smooth flow of a jump or a trick.

Differentiation

A freestyler achieves optimal precision of movement through differentiation of individual phases of movement such as takeoff, flight, and landing, as well as body movements such as pulling up the legs. It is the basis for enhanced expressiveness, which is possible only with high consistency of movement. Good differentiation also exerts a great influence on economy of movement in Freestyle. This fact should not be underestimated with respect to the physical demands (see Physical Performance Factors) posed by a run in the halfpipe or in overall training.

Balance

Balance is an elementary requirement in Freestyle. Its quality is evident in every move in this sport. The body is kept in balance through moves (e.g., the support phase of a hand plant); during and after extensive body movements (e.g., spin tricks), balance is maintained or reestablished, for example, upon landing.

Orientation

Demands on orientation skills increase in proportion to the complexity of tricks and jumps. Their development is an important prerequisite for moves executed around several body axes. This is evident even with simple tricks and hits. It's clear that there is a close relationship here to linking and timing. Freestylers must have the ability to control and change the position and movements of the body in relation to the ground or transition.

Good orientation ability also becomes an important safety factor in the execution of a move. A secure landing depends greatly on this skill.

The great demands on technique and coordination in Freestyle are evident in both phases of the McTwist.

Rhythmizing

A freestyler's rhythmizing is noticeable in how the approach, takeoff, flight, and landing are strung together.

This skill is evident especially in the order of moves, their harmony, and their expression, such as with an entire run in the halfpipe. Rhythmic technique also plays a role in Freeriding on the slope and in Boardercross racing.

Reaction

This ability was already addressed in the section on speed. Relative to the timing of movements and to the most effective instant, reaction is a determining factor in performance. It includes adjusting movement speed to the situation. In Freestyle, speed is usually wide-open (see Reaction Speed).

Adjustment

A freestyler's ability to adjust to changing external conditions is very important. These include changing snow and visibility conditions as well as the use of new board materials or a different halfpipe configuration.

The sudden introduction of new circumstances necessitates consistency of technique. That means that the freestyler's flexibility doesn't interfere with performance, and it becomes another safety factor in relation to falls and injuries.

Psychological Performance Factors

It seems that these performance factors are continually taking on more importance in Freestyle, as evidenced by the development of competitions (especially halfpipe). The sharply increasing degree of difficulty and the complexity of moves (e.g., automated performance of an entire run in the halfpipe) pose extremely high demands on psychological skills. Concentration on the run in a halfpipe competition and waiting for the start are major stress factors. There is also an unmistakable increase in the pressure to perform at top levels. Fear of bad falls or injuries is a further psychological stress factor that often produces stagnation in technique. These developments make obvious the necessary integration of psychological performance factors into Freestyle training. The objectives for improving this factor can turn out very differently among several riders.

Concentration and willpower are an important factor at the start of Boardercross.

Equipment and Material Factors

Equipment and material factors can play a role in supporting and developing a freerider's technique. They are counted among the external performance factors. Based on their immense significance to technique they will be addressed separately at this time. The significance of board technology for Freestyle has already been addressed several times. Different uses and physiques require different board materials for achieving the best possible technique in carrying out movements. Still, riders must adapt themselves to the equipment. Yet another important aspect is the choice of board, binding, and boot combination. These elements should complement one another and be matched precisely as possible to their intended use.

Equipment and materials technology is constantly subject to further development. Therefore, as riders progress in their technique and place new demands on their equipment, and as new advances become available in the marketplace, the need to upgrade will be practically unavoidable. Riders who wish to remain competitive and to perform at their highest level will replace their equipment regularly, not because it has worn out, but rather because it has been eclipsed. Serious riders will remain apprised of changes in equipment technology by contact with trainers and other riders, by visiting pro shops, and by reading current periodical literature.

Gloves provide an important protective function in Freestyle. Strain on the palms and wrists can be severe. Specially reinforced gloves with form-fitting wrist protectors should be provided for this type of use. In the interest of safety it is likewise recommended to wear a skateboarding helmet while learning difficult hits.

External Performance Factors

External performance factors can be performance-limiting as well as performance-enhancing qualities. Both properties can even appear as a single factor.

That depends on the respective level of the rider. So, for example, a very good freestyler can improve coordination under conditions of somewhat reduced visibility. For a beginning freestyler, on the other hand, training under these conditions could hinder technique or even be dangerous.

The most important external factors include
- Composition of the halfpipe, obstacle course, Boardercross run, or jump
- Snow conditions
- Visibility
- Temperature
- Wind
- Opponents (in Boardercross)
- Spectators

The presence of determining conditions or their regular incorporation into training is an important element in overall training methodology.

Spectators have a decisive effect on some riders.

Tactical Performance Factors

Freestylers' tactical skills lie in the control of their movements under competition conditions.

The ability to concentrate is decisive in this case. In Boardercross there's also the need to anticipate how to act in relation to the opponents.

YEAR-ROUND TRAINING

Precision in jumps is greatly influenced by speed.

The trend to year-round improvement of specific skills is identifiable even in Freestyle and corresponds to development of performance. Beyond our winter season, training camps are conducted on glaciers in spring or summer, and there are competitions in the southern hemisphere. On-snow training is possible depending on available time. These camps offer first of all lots of fun and motivation for training; secondly, they allow riders to train with others and to learn new styles or techniques.

But even without this on-snow training there are a number of possibilities to improve general and specific skills (see p. 103). In any case this should provide preparation for the real season.

A yearlong training plan for Freestyle should follow the principles of Periodic and Cyclic Training (see pp. 16 and 18). Training over the entire year or even a longer period should be based on the method already mentioned (see p. 33).

Training for General Conditioning

Improvement in general endurance, strength, speed, and agility is an important base for winter training in Freestyle. Anyone who fails to develop them during the summer will feel it by the beginning of the winter.

The following observations are extensions of existing thorough explanations from racing that refer to training methods for conditioning.

General Endurance

General endurance should receive a little more attention at the start of preparations for the winter. At that time there is still ample time to devote to developing endurance. Mountain biking, running, and in-line skating are very good for this. During the competition season this training has a regenerative character (e.g., relaxed runs).

General Strength

Strength training, especially development of jumping ability, is crucial to Freestyle training. Freestylers can improve their jumping ability dramatically by following the methods presented in the chapter on racing (see p. 38ff.).

This is especially important for riders who don't have too much jumping ability (inherent talent).

Training for jumping ability should be carried out year-round. The intensity should increase substantially throughout the winter and decrease a bit from after the competitive season to the start of preparation for the following winter.

General Speed

Speed training is closely linked to training for jumping ability. This involves improving action and reaction time of body movements. In addition to the methods mentioned in the racing section, there are other specific possibilities in sports with similar movements. These include

- Trampoline work (with no board)
- In-line skating in halfpipe
- Skateboarding
- Water bounding (without board)

The improvement in speed through these sports depends greatly on the freestyler's ability in the chosen sport. Learning and practicing one or more of these sports is therefore recommended.

Development of Freestyle-specific speed is addressed by the contents of the on-snow training and in every technique workout during the competitive season.

Agility

The importance of agility and its preventive effect on susceptibility to injury has been made abundantly clear in the sections on Performance in Freestyle and Racing. Possible methods were likewise described there (see p. 45). Yet the freestyler should emphasize agility even more than the racer, since it controls performance in Freestyle even more.

Increased agility and agility training involve the following body parts:

- Neck and neck muscles
- Shoulder joints and muscles
- Back and back muscles
- Hip joints and muscles
- Wrists and arms muscles
- Knees and ankles and all leg muscles

At this point studies (e.g., by Anderson) should be referred to as they pertain to year-round, regular agility programs conducted before and after training.

IMPORTANT TRAINING TIPS FOR YOUNG FREESTYLERS

Freestyle places great stress not only on the board material, but also on the human body. Young freestylers should pay particular attention to this fact. Young snowboarders possess the best requirement for the Freestyle discipline: their own bodies. Riders who build their bodies wisely and give them time to develop will experience Freestyle to the fullest and discover their own style. That's how to expand the possibilities and enjoy the sport for a long time before reaching the body's limits. The following information is intended to make this fact as clear as possible to young freestylers.

A Body Develops Only One Time

Every freestyler develops differently. This is true for body development too. The basis for this development process is created in childhood and in adolescence. For the young freestyler there is an interesting period between the ages of six or seven to eighteen or nineteen.

Stresses

During this period the body experiences several growth phases. This affects bone growth in particular. The skeleton is completely mature at the end of this period, but before that time it cannot withstand too much stress. Higher pressure and tension stresses are therefore possible only after the end of this development process.

Excessive stresses, especially on the spinal column, are to be avoided, since they can lead to bone deformations, growth interruptions, chest deformities, and reduced agility.

But young snowboarders are subject to these stresses. They are often exaggerated by unsound training methods and by excessive ambition. Another major stress factor is represented by the accumulation of athletic injuries.

Youngsters must force themselves to eliminate injuries. If they neglect that, there's no guarantee they won't experience considerable interference with their physical abilities.

Young freestylers definitely should watch out for the following threats of stress and injury:

Freestyle, an opportunity for young snowboarders; but bodies develop just once.

- Training too soon after an injury interferes with further healing, dramatically restricts technique, or even distorts it.
- Oftentimes there is also an element of fear. Fear means faulty execution of moves and heightened danger of injury. This turns into a vicious circle.
- Many hits are comprised of several turns. These turns are produced by torque of the body (see p. 102). Not only the body and its mass must be applied to the turn, but also the additional mass of the snowboard.

Especially upon poor initiation and execution of the turn movement, this can lead to enormous stresses, particularly to the spine. If these moves are repeated in the same way, injuries are unavoidable.

General overestimation of one's technical skills can lead to considerable stress to the entire body or even to injuries. This is most evident in landings on level terrain, since they subject the body to tremendous strain. Falls are not uncommon in such instances.

Another stress factor lies within the board. Young freestylers who choose a board that does not match their physique and skills expose themselves to increased physical stresses.

The great interest of young snowboarders in Freestyle is understandable. The motivation to do Freestyle is a tremendously important factor in success. But at this age too much of one thing can often mean an excessive increase in physical stress. With that in mind, the following advice is offered to young freestylers:

Injuries must always be healed thoroughly. Only after this process should training be resumed.

Hits with turn movements should be handled carefully. They should be learned only when physical and technical requirements are satisfactory. Since physical development occurs differently in everyone, stresses should be adjusted individually. Steps in the learning process should be slow and detailed. False ambition is inappropriate in the face of fear. People don't have to prove themselves in front of friends.

Ambition and motivation should always exist in relationship to one's ability. Heightened risk aversion and conscious execution of tricks and hits are a good defense against painful surprises. Also, training with friends should not degenerate into ill-considered tests of strength.

Today's board technology offers the appropriate board for every ability level, every application, and every individual physique.

Before purchasing a board young freestylers should, if possible, try out several of the boards they are considering, or at least gather as much information as possible. This avoids use of ineffective and inappropriate equipment.

There is only one remedy for one-sidedness and the attendant danger of strain: versatility. Young freestylers especially should not limit themselves to snowboarding as they accumulate movement experience. The more sports they try, the more versatile their movement potential becomes, and the more fun they have in Freestyle.

Unique Opportunities

Young freestylers have unique opportunities to develop jumping ability, speed, and agility. This is no exaggeration. The conditions for developing these elementary Freestyle skills are at their best during youth. Anyone who misses this time will not be able to develop to the fullest.

This chance applies also to technique and coordination (see p. 86). As an example, children between the ages of seven and twelve have outstanding abilities for acquiring Freestyle-specific techniques.

Well-developed coordination is a requirement for continued learning, refinement, stabilization, and application of technique and for economical use of physical conditioning.

TECHNIQUE TRAINING

Movement Perception and Concept of Movement

The basis of good moves for freestylers broadens their movement perception and concept of movement. Developing and refining these qualities is not only a requirement for successful performance of moves, but also the root of style and expressiveness in moves.

Movement perception and a concept of movement are important components of motor learning (see p. 52). Every freestyler perceives moves through the sense organs, in which the information conveyed by individual analyzers (see p. 26) lead to a mirror imaging of how the move is performed. This includes unconscious perception among beginners and conscious (and therefore verbally reproducible) perception among experienced riders.

Conception of movement starts as a thought about how to perform a move. It becomes more clearly defined through meaningful perception and accumulation of movement experiences. In the verbal account the freestyler can differentiate among spatial, temporal, and dynamic qualities and their relationships to one another.

Complex moves require systematic training.

Freestyle poses extremely high demands on snowboarders' coordination. Observation of moves and combinations makes that evident. How can a snowboarder who's interested in Freestyle pick up that variety of movement and put it to best use?

The following explanations are a possible answer to that question. At this juncture there are many roads that lead to the goal. But this one is certain: The continuing development in technique makes systematic technique training increasingly necessary to experience success.

Spatial, temporal, and dynamic movement qualities that figure in the verbal account:

Spatial qualities:
Place, direction, and degree of shifting of body parts with respect to one another, and the body's shift in surrounding space (e.g., describing the arching used in a back flip).

Temporal qualities:
Time, duration, and speed of sequential or simultaneous movements of body parts in relation to one another and to the shifting of the body in surrounding space (e.g., the precise moment when a grab is performed).

Movement perception and conception accompany freestylers from the beginning of their technical development. They influence the quality of technique. The goal of training should therefore be ongoing refinement and development of this most important element of technique.

Basic Structure of Freestyle-specific Moves

The basic structure of tricks and hits can usually be described by dividing it into three segments: preparation, main part, and conclusion. These three phases exist in a very definite relationship to each other, and the following considerations apply:

- Their sequence cannot be changed.
- They are not interchangeable.
- Changes in these structures destroy the unity and the purpose of the move.

The function of the preparation phase generally consists of creating the best conditions for successful and economical execution of the main phase. The preparation phase is comprised of the approach and

Approach and takeoff—preparation stage.

Main part of the move.

Preparation for landing and landing, with conclusion.

A handplant in the support phase divides the first and second flight phases (jumping onto support, and flight phase after support, respectively).

The relationship between the preparation and main phases makes it clear how closely linked the phases are. The preparation phase, such as executing the takeoff, is defined by how the move in the main phase is carried out. The timing of the hit is therefore just as important as the direction of approach, such as the angle of approach on the wall, or the nature of the takeoff point (e.g., high or low rise to the jump). The performance of the move in the main or flight phase is determined in large measure by the quality of the approach in the preparation phase.

There are some important considerations between the main and final phases of a move. Especially in the halfpipe the final phase or landing contributes to the success of the following move. But the final phase is determined by how the main phase turns out. So, for example, opening the body too early or too late in a spin trick carries over to the quality of the landing, and consequently to subsequent moves.

The three basic phases can be further divided with respect to their individual actions. The component parts of the preparation phase are

- Approach on toe or heel side
- Approach head-on or backward
- Angle of approach (steep or shallow)
- Takeoff from very low position

the takeoff. The takeoff is usually accomplished by bending in the hip, knee, and ankle areas, and in part by swinging the arms back.

The move is actually performed in the main phase. In the case of hits, it constitutes a flight phase. With handplants, the flight phase is divided by the support phase into a first and a second flight phase. In the main phase, freestylers impart movement to their whole bodies and use it efficiently. Additionally, the mass of the board must be accelerated by this impulse.

The final phase usually begins at a specific point at which the freestyler's body is still in rapid movement or in a delicate state of balance. During the landing, great muscle strength is needed to slow down the body, as in cushioning by bending the knees deeply. Another trait of the final phase involves transitioning to a new preparation phase for the next move, as in the halfpipe.

Within the flight phase there are some apparently free-standing movements, such as turns around the long and diagonal axes of the body. The shifts and turns in the flight phase are not, however, separate movements, but elements that are integrated into the overall move. The individual elements serve a preparatory function for the ones that follow.

The separate preparatory moves deserve further explanation. An example is arm movements to initiate turns around the body's long axis.

There are some important and necessary movements at the end of a flight phase, such as opening up the hit in preparation for the landing.

The final phase can be divided into the following with respect to the landing:

- Landing on the entire surface of the board
- Landing forward or backward in direction of travel

Connecting Movements

In Freestyle a lot of impetus is needed to execute moves; that's accomplished only through cooperation among big muscle groups and through movements in the extremities, the torso, and the head (e.g., turning the head). These movements usually don't occur simultaneously, but rather sequentially.

Freestylers should strive to connect these movements as smoothly as possible with respect to timing, extent of movement, and utilization of strength. Swinging the arms, for example, or moving the torso, thus connects to the takeoff movement in the legs.

The connecting of all movements is influenced by the mechanical properties of the movement apparatus. It is subject to biomechanical laws and to the mechanisms that control coordination. Some factors in connecting movements will next be explained since they are important in performing Freestyle moves.

Clearly shown are linking between takeoff and turning the torso with respect to the legs in a spin.

Right after takeoff the McTwist phase illustrates the swing transfer of the torso and arms on the legs and the board.

Swing Transfer

Many tricks and hits are executed by swinging the arms. This applies especially to takeoff. At the start of the takeoff, the applicable limbs are accelerated explosively in the takeoff direction. A high initial velocity is imparted to the center of gravity of the limbs while the speed of the torso lags behind. The swinging movement is slowed by the muscles just before the board breaks loose from the surface. The swing is thus only partly communicated to the torso. Differences in timing of the swing transfer are evident between beginners and advanced riders. Clear, resilient swing moves are less common among beginners. With jumps that are produced by swing transfer, the acceleration of the body's center of gravity is amplified significantly, as in the case of crouching deeply before the takeoff. In addition, greater height is imparted to the center of gravity by a straightening movement at the start of the flight phase, and that has a positive effect on the flight path.

Temporal Displacement of Moves

It's easy to see the sequencing of movements or actions in almost all Freestyle moves by watching video clips in slow motion. Sequencing can also be seen at normal speed.

The flight phase is usually initiated with the head, the arms, and the torso. While these parts are already engaged in the main phase of performing a move, the legs are still in the preparation phase (straightening the legs upon takeoff). The temporal displacement continues through the last link in this chain of movement. It concerns the part of the chain that is located on the support side of the body and imparts takeoff momentum to the entire body. Upon takeoff these are the legs and feet; with handplants, the arms and hands.

Significance of Using the Torso

Moving the torso plays an essential role in linking movements in Freestyle, since the torso has greater mass than the other body parts. The type and manner of acceleration, the movement of this mass, and its application to the entire move often determine the quality of a hit or a trick.

Additionally the torso is an important part in transferring movement impulses to other body parts (see pp. 97, 102). So, for example, a rotation can be transferred to the legs and the board only by the torso. Another important function of the torso is the directional start in temporal displacement of moves, for instance, in turning the torso relative to the legs and board in the direction of travel in a spin trick (such as five-forties).

The torso can be used in the following ways:
- vertical or horizontal, e.g., straightening torso in takeoff
- in rotation, e.g., in all spin tricks for transfer of turn impulse to the legs and board
- Bending/stretching or arching, e.g., in back flips
- Twisting, e.g., in turning the torso over the legs

These movements usually don't appear in isolation in Freestyle, but rather are mixed together.

Steering Function of the Head

A fundamental in executing moves in Freestyle involves coordinating the connecting of component moves of the head with the movements of the torso and the limbs. Visual orientation is an essential factor in the head's importance in steering. The direction of movement or the landing are fixed in the vision, even before the body heads for the target or the change in direction is executed.

Use of the torso in rotation is evident upon takeoff in a handplant.

In rotations, visual orientation contributes greatly to safe, effective steering and control of the overall move. The landing spot is picked out as quickly as possible, or especially with multiple rotations (e.g., 720°), a point of reference is kept in sight as long as possible, and then another or the same one is picked up again.

The importance of head movement for the overall move is illustrated by another fact. Reflexes associated with the neck muscles are triggered by the initial head movements. These reflexes cause an increase in tension in certain functionally related muscle groups. So tipping the head back, for example, as in a back flip, causes an increase in tension in the back muscles or the arm muscles. That's how a strong takeoff, maximum arching in a back flip, or a powerful impression is achieved with the arm(s) in a handplant.

Tipping the head raises the tension in muscles of the torso (e.g., stomach muscles). This is especially important for turns in a crouch, such as a McTwist.

Further Observations on Movement

Further observations on movement technique in Freestyle concern

- Types of movement
- Axes of rotation
- Body axes
- Center of gravity
- Flight path
- Triggering of turning movements
- Changing of turn speed

Types of Movements

Movements in Freestyle can be divided into so-called progressive (translation movements) and rotation or turning movements.

Pure progressive movements are, for example, straight hits off a jump. These types of moves also appear in mixed form. So, for example, a spin trick consists of a rotation component and a progressive component in the direction of flight (see Fig. 14).

Turn Axes

The point around which a body turns is known as a turning point or spin axis. Here a distinction can be made in Freestyle tricks and hits between temporarily fixed and free axes of spin (e.g., takeoff or support phase of arms in handplants, as in Fig.15; and flight phase in all hits, as in Fig.16, respectively).

Both forms of axis can appear in combination in a trick. So, for example, the first main phase of a handplant may consist of a free spin axis (unsupported phase). It concludes with a support phase that has a temporarily fixed axis, which is now superseded by a free axis in the second main phase. With respect to the body there are three axes around which turns can be performed.

Fig. 14: A spin trick
consists of a rotation
and a progressive
component.

Fig. 15: A temporarily
fixed spin axis is
used in handplants in
the support phase.

Fig. 16: Free spin axes always occur in the flight phase of a jump.

Axes of the Body

For a better understanding of movement of the body around axes, it is necessary to have a look at the spatial axes of the human body. The stance on the board makes it harder to visualize the axes of spin. That's why it's especially important for freestylers to know their spin axes while stationary on their boards and to differentiate among them.

Freestylers have three body axes at their disposal. They are

- The long axis of the body
- The broad axis
- The through axis

The body axes are very important to Freestyle. While the first two are often used singly or in combination, the through axis occurs only rarely in connection with turns.

The long axis (see Fig. 17) runs from the midpoint of the head down to a point between the feet. Most turn moves, especially in the halfpipe, follow this axis. That includes not only spin, trick, and invert variations, but also all straight hits. They entail a fairly emphatic turn around the long axis in order to reach the transition.

Another form of turn movements that involve this axis are the so-called twists. In these moves the torso and legs twist in reverse direction and compensate for one another.

Fig. 17: The body's long and through axes.

The broad axis (see Fig. 18) runs through the hips. This axis is an especially complex one in mental imaging for moves, since it makes it possible to change the direction of the turn based on the position of the pelvis over the board. The following turn directions are dependent on the position of the freestyler's pelvis over the board:

Fig. 18: The body's broad axis.

- With frontal position of pelvis facing the nose (body leaning toward nose) and tail (arching or leaning toward tail)
- With sideways position of pelvis facing toeside (body leaning toward toeside) and heelside (arching toward heelside)

The through axis (see Fig. 17) runs through the body from front to rear. It can be used as a turning axis if it's in a very lateral position, but it is of secondary importance in turning movements.

Center of Gravity and Gravitational Pull

Freestylers always have to deal with gravity in hits and tricks. At first glance this may seem self-evident, but in many cases this criterion is given short shrift in practice. The center of gravity conceived of as an arithmetic center of body mass is of great importance. The center of gravity in many movements can even lie outside the body. Gravity always acts upon it. Gravity can produce no turning movements by itself. Therefore, every initial turning movement is carried through in free flight.

Flight Paths

The importance of gravitational pull on the center of gravity as just mentioned becomes particularly clear in the flight path of hits. The center of gravity describes a parabolic flight path.

The flight path is determined largely by
- Location of the center of gravity just before takeoff
- Approach speed
- Freestyler's jumping strength and timing at takeoff
- Direction of approach
- Angle of takeoff
- Height of wall or jump
- Pitch of slope in landing zone of halfpipe or jump

All these criteria are closely connected to one another and influence each other.

The center of gravity is changed by an explosive straightening of the legs at takeoff and produces a position favorable to the flight path. After takeoff, movement in the center of gravity consists of

- A constant, horizontal movement that is dictated by the nature of the jump or wall; the approach speed; and with steep jumps or walls, also by the takeoff
- A vertical component, which likewise depends on the approach speed and raising the center of gravity by straightening the legs and torso

The higher a jump or a wall, the shorter the flight distance and the greater the altitude through displacement of center of gravity (horizontally toward the rear by straightening the legs on takeoff). This situation is of major importance in performing flips.

As already explained, the approach speed has a great influence on the height, distance, and duration of a jump. Closely bound to the approach speed is timing at takeoff. The higher the speed in the approach, the sooner the takeoff.

The strength of the jump has an essential bearing on positioning the center of gravity at takeoff. After takeoff, the center of gravity can no longer be changed before landing on the preestablished flight path. This fact is often forgotten. Therefore freestylers should train seriously for the takeoff.

The direction of approach at the takeoff point is especially crucial in the halfpipe. In contrast to hits, where the approach is always in a downhill direction, the approach on the wall is always handled differently (see Fig. 19). Freestylers have many possible takeoff moves. According to body position, the takeoff impulse drops and consequently the flight path of the body's center of gravity is variable.

The takeoff angle is a function of the pitch of the wall or jump, plus the angle of approach on the wall. The takeoff angle can be very shallow, as with a flat jump, but also very steep in the case of a frontal approach on a perpendicular wall.

The height of the jump or halfpipe wall and the slope of the landing zone are decisive factors in duration of flight. The greater these parameters, the longer the duration of a hit. The downhill flight path is lengthened as the pitch of the slope increases.

These considerations are significant in performing multiple spins, or high and long straight hits (big airs) with lots of grab variations, since the moves can be of higher quality, given the longer flight time. Longer flight time can also produce better style.

Experimenting with different approach speeds and angles, plus variations in take-off angle, will show what works best for specific airs. Differences in body weight, physique, conditioning, and equipment mean that we can not draw precise conclusions that apply to all riders. But purposeful training and a clear conception of the body's axes during flight can help all freestylers discover what works best for them.

Triggering Turning Movements

The triggering of turning movements is based on forces that work on the center of gravity. Torque, which is necessary for starting rotation, is achieved in the following ways, depending on the jump:

- Turning the torso in the direction of the turn (thereby producing a turn around the long axis of the body)
- Arching toward the tail to produce a turn along the broad axis in direction of tail
- Arching toward the nose to produce a turn around the broad axis in direction of nose
- Arching toward heelside to effect a turn along broad axis toward heelside
- Arching toward toeside to turn along broad axis in toeside direction

With turns around the long axis, the upper body is bent a little toward the turning side and turned with respect to the legs (see photo at top of p. 103). With turns around the broad axis, the body is arched to produce the torque.

Fig. 19: Different flight paths according to center of gravity (CG) in conjunction with angle of approach on the wall.

The legs and board are still locked in the direction of the turn because of the continuing contact of the board on the snow.

This condition is similar to a compressed spring. The position and the distance between bindings play an important part in this. The farther apart the bindings are on the board, the stronger the torque that can be applied to compressing the spring, and the more turns that can be made because of the high turning force. With a weak binding position (diagonally on the board), a stronger twisting of torso and legs is possible just before takeoff (see photo at bottom p. 103). The spring can thus be compressed even more tightly.

The binding position and the distance between bindings is, however, also matched to the rider's physique and riding habits. Freestylers should experiment with both of these parameters until they find the best individual arrangement.

Once the board loses contact with the snow after takeoff, legs and board follow the direction of movement of the head and body. Freestylers maintain the initial turning impulse with their board; they cannot pull their body and board out of the flight path determined at takeoff.

Turns are slowed down by a controlled opening or stretching of the body before landing.

Changing Turning Speed

Freestylers can make their bodies turn faster by pulling in their arms and legs closer to the turn axis (e.g., by bending the legs). Conversely, the farther the body parts are from the axis of turn, the slower the body turns. In almost straight somersaults such as back flips, freestylers turn as slowly as possible along their broad axis. With the same turning impulse they can get one turn around this axis out of a straight body position, and up to three in a crouch. The mass and especially the length of the board are very important considerations in this instance.

Especially in turns around the long body axis, long boards make the spin more difficult. Board choice is therefore of great importance.

Turning the upper body relative to the legs creates a situation on takeoff that is analogous to a compressed spring.

Changing turns speed therefore depends on
- Distance of body parts from axis of rotation
- Board choice (see p. 111)

Here are some further conclusions about technique that can be drawn from the aforementioned:
- A high number of turns in the flight phase and their best execution is possible because of these considerations.
- Conscious slowing down or acceleration of turns is extremely important for a controlled flight phase as well as for a safe landing.
- Because of their possible variations in execution, turn moves offer freestylers an opportunity to develop and refine their style.

General Technique Training

Good technique in Freestyle is based on general coordination (see p. 86). This can be improved in many ways through other types of sports, especially off-season. Possibilities include
- Skateboarding
- In-line skating
- Surfing
- Mountain biking
- Trampoline jumping
- Water bounding
- Underwater training
- Indoor circuit training

Agility training should always be conducted in conjunction with these workout possibilities. Aside from improved coordination, these sports provide a welcome change that motivates and produces new ideas on style. You have to expand your horizons to continue developing your expressiveness through movement.

BMX: a possibility for improving coordination and conditioning off-season.

Introduction to Performing Moves

At all levels of achievement an introduction to performing moves can take place under modified and simplified conditions. By this we don't mean simplified conditions in on-snow training, but rather a preliminary step toward that. Freestylers can gain first contacts with similar moves in other types of sports that offer easier conditions, which later can be performed on the board.

These conditions are found especially in trampoline work, water bounding, underwater training, and indoor circuit training. Without the hindrance of a board strapped to their feet, freestylers can concentrate fully on their moves. Underwater training is one of the easiest methods to improve spatial orientation. Conditions here are simplified as much as possible. Freestylers dive into a pool and try to turn around the individual body axes. This provides a good simulation of the turning mechanisms, their order in time, and their position in space. An advantage of this training is its minimal expense.

Jumping on a minitrampoline on a soft floor mat involves an important forward motion that exists also in training on snow. Jumping on a big trampoline and water bounding offer only a little of this forward- or backward-directed component (backward somersaults). Minitrampoline also makes it possible to use

the help of friends or cushions of mats. A full-size trampoline can be a help too when a safety belt is used.

In so-called indoor training circuits, stations are set up that include such important movements as

- Balanced landings on both feet
- Jumping moves
- Rotations

Here there are no limits imposed on how simulations are conceived. The circuit can also be viewed as a run in a halfpipe, where at each station a new move is presented as a trick or a jump as the circuit is run through. This encourages not only coordination but also accumulation of moves.

The goal of this type of training is to collect new experiences in movement:

- For takeoff:
  Approach speed, takeoff intensity (speed in straightening legs)
- For flight path:
  Feeling for how one's body behaves during the jump, influence of takeoff angle on flight path
- For landing:
  Body position upon landing
- For connecting moves:
  Steering with the head, arching the body, turning the torso, straightening or pulling up the legs
- For various axes of rotation:
  Turns around the long body axis to left and right (screw turns), turns around the broad axis forward and backward (somersaults), turns around the through axis (lateral somersaults)
- For changing speed in turns:
  Crouching and extended somersaults, pulling in arms in screw-turn movements
- For temporal-spatial orientation:
  Steering with the head, conscious opening of the body in landing a somersault on the trampoline

Possibilities for improving Freestyle-specific movements:

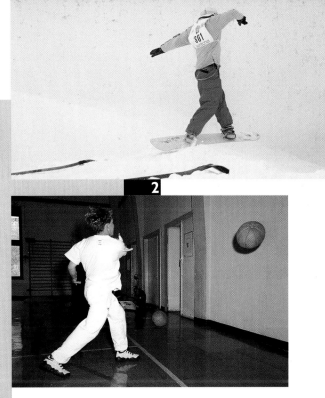

Improving dynamics of movement by turning during takeoff

Jumping ability and balance training

Arranging the body in stable position for landing

Coordination of turning movement during flight phase

Freestylers should never risk too much in this training. Observe the general rules for training: from the easy to the difficult, and from the simple to the complex.

Riders should slowly develop a feel for the movements (even with training devices in place) by starting with simple moves and by slowly increasing the difficulty. The following applies especially to beginners:

- Attempt hits without turns (e.g., stretch hits) before jumps with simple hits
- Attempt simple turns before multiple turns

These fundamentals pertain to all axes of rotation. When sufficient consistency is established in the moves, the degree of difficulty can be raised. Generally training should entail no anxiety, but even with minitrampoline, trampoline, or water bounding there is a danger of injury.

In any case, freestylers should do this training with friends or with the coach. That has advantages for safety as well as for talking about the moves as friends observe them.

Training should be continued during the season. Here the principle of balance applies too. Training that's too one-sided and that involves no on-snow training has some disadvantages: frequently the moves cannot be transferred to the more difficult conditions on snow, so they hinder further progress.

Goals of Special Technique Training

Special training for technique involves on-snow training. It includes essentially the following five training emphases:

- Riding technique
- Takeoff phase
- Flight phase
- Landing phase
- Style

Freestylers should train deliberately for these five emphases from the beginning of their training. The training goals formulated earlier (see p. 81) play an essential role in this. The five emphases take on major significance as technique develops.

Training for Riding Technique

Riding technique is an elementary requirement in Freestyle. Unfortunately, this fact is often underestimated. This performance factor is essential for secure and controlled completion of tricks and jumps in the halfpipe. That's where faulty technique can be seen as the cause for an unsuccessful outcome. Riding technique becomes even more important in Boardercross racing, which demands of the rider enormous technical skills as well as jumping ability. The most important aspect of good riding technique from a personal point of view is the fun and motivation it provides in doing Freestyle.

When possible, training should be done with a group of friends or with a coach. That way it's easier to talk about how the moves are done, and training duties can be arranged better. Training on your own requires lots of persistence and patience. You also need a willingness to carry through moves by yourself and to work hard.

Improvement in riding technique should result from technique training in races, as already described. That's how freestylers improve their technique and simultaneously prepare for the technical elements of Boardercross. Riders who line up for racing as well as Freestyle disciplines should train with the appropriate equipment.

For pure freestylers, pole training with a Freestyle-board is recommended. Additionally, specific technique training should be conducted to include the following:

- Riding in the halfpipe (wall to wall)
- Freeriding on the slope

The goals for riding in the halfpipe apply only to riding and not to jumping; they include:

- Maintaining a central position (both legs evenly weighted)
- Controlled weighting of the heelside edge
- Anticipating the turning point on the wall
- Controlling weighting and unweighting at turning point on the wall
- Assuming a low body position through the flats
- Rhythmic and harmonic riding wall to wall (calm, controlled manner)

- Riding different approach angles
- Performing the mentioned items while gliding backward (fakie)
- Alternating riding direction during the run in accordance with the mentioned items
- Pretending a change in riding direction (reaction and concentration training)

Riding on the trail likewise is suited to experimenting with changes in weighting and in body position.

This includes:

- Riding all types of turns with different radii and under different snow and terrain conditions

- Riding fakie variations with different radii and under different snow and terrain conditions
- Developing basic maneuvers such as Tail Wheelies, Laybackslides, Ollies (with and without grab variations), Noserolls (180° and greater) and Tail Rolls (180° and greater)

Freeriding offers yet another possibility for improving riding technique and for increasing motivation. That's where freestylers find the most demanding conditions and have to have their riding technique in good order.

In all of these possibilities for improving riding technique the fundamental of individuality occupies an exalted position. Naturally this pertains also to riding style. There is no right or wrong here. Riding style is developed according to the observations already presented in the racing section (see p. 61). There are also differences in equipment technology (see p. 111).

Training for Takeoff

Takeoff, flight, and landing phases (preparation, main, and final phases) are closely connected to one another. On-snow training always includes all three. Freestylers should, however, be in a position to emphasize one of these three phases in their training.

Good riding technique is a basic requirement for learning all hits.

Here training for takeoff will be examined separately from the other two phases. It takes on a special significance. Its main features are:

- Approach technique
- Building up of pressure
- Generation of torque (turning impulse)
- Head steering
- Optimal connecting of movements and timing of takeoff

Approach Technique:

The approach to the jump depends on the preparation of the takeoff zone. Generally the approach is made in a low body position with upright head facing the direction of travel.

With respect to preparation of the takeoff zone, there are these differences:

- Approach in the fall line on a jump
- Oblique approach on the wall in a halfpipe
- Frontal approach on the wall in a halfpipe

In an approach to a jump in the fall line the entire board is weighted as evenly as possible. This is possible only on tracks that don't lean to one side or the other. The same is true for the last approach segment, the frontal approach on the wall in the halfpipe.

A special form of this approach technique exists in the halfpipe with approaches on the wall. These are similar to jumps and appear steepest at the top. A flat board position is often possible in such cases. In an oblique approach to the wall, the wall-side board edge will always be weighted more or less as already explained, according to the approach angle.

Pressure Buildup:

Pressure buildup is guided by movements in the flight phase. It is produced from a low body position by explosively straightening the legs, hips, and torso over:

- The whole board surface
- The toe- or heelside
- The board edge
- The tail
- The nose

In straight hits off a jump, pressure should be applied to the entire board surface. This is possible only on takeoff zones that don't tip to the side. With

Pressure buildup in the takeoff is crucial to height and quality of the flight phase, as shown here in a takeoff from a handplant.

hits that involve turns, the pressure is applied according to the direction of the turn:

- Over the toe- or heelside edge (all spins along the long axis of the body, e.g., seven-twenties)
- Over the tail (e.g., backflips)
- Over the nose (e.g., flips in fakie variations at takeoff)

In halfpipes the pressure buildup is often exerted on the wall-side board edge. This applies especially for spin tricks on the long axis of the body, and to straight hits. Combination forms of jumping pressure are present in spins or handplants around the body's broad axis. In this case, besides the pressure on the wall-side board edge, there is an additional pressure buildup over the tail (as with a McTwist) or over the nose (e.g., Elguerial Handplant) which is produced by shifting the weight onto the leg that is closer to the transition.

Producing Torque:

Creating torque is fundamental to many jumps. It is generally subject to the mechanisms that have already been described thoroughly (see p. 102). Torso and head initiate the desired movement for the flight.

Head Steering:

Upon takeoff freestylers orient themselves by turning or tipping the head forward or backward in the resulting direction of movement.

This action during takeoff is basic (see p. 98). Leaving it out makes it hard to accomplish in subsequent moves.

Head steering, connecting movements, and takeoff timing set up the movements for a figure during the flight phase.

Optimizing Connecting of Movements and Takeoff Timing:

The importance of the takeoff is made clear by the number of its component moves. But the difficulty of the takeoff lies not just in the number of movements that comprise it, but also in linking them together, and in the timing.

The component moves are best connected through

- Deliberate and frequent repetitions or exercises
- Mental imaging
- Verbalization about the movements with friends or coach
- Observation of other riders or demonstration videos

Takeoff timing can be improved by using markers, by having friends shout to the rider, and by practicing a lot. It's easier to improve timing by using consistent rather than variable approach speeds.

Movements during the flight phase can be improved by using methods of general technique training.

Training for Flight and Landing Phases

The interdependence of all three move phases becomes especially clear in the flight and landing phases.

The quality of the flight phase determines how good the landing is. That's why the two phases are always trained for together. Training for moves during the flight phase should be guided as much as possible by measures from overall technique training (e.g., trampoline work and indoor training circuits), by observations of other riders, and by analysis of video shots that illustrate the appropriate movements. This applies especially to the acquisition of new moves. Here too it's important to analyze the moves deliberately with friends or with the coach.

At this point the basics for learning new moves (i.e., from the easy to the difficult, from the simple to the complex), which have already been mentioned several times, are extremely important with regard to safety and risk of injury. They must be included without fail.

For hits and tricks, this means specifically:

- Maintain control on takeoff
- Slowly develop a feel for new moves
- Learn straight hits before spin tricks
- Increase the height of jumps slowly (control approach speed)

- Inverts are first done in a crouch, then straight
- Grab variations and style should be worked on only after the basic movement has been mastered (also with inverts)
- Simple spins must be mastered safely before doing multiple spins
- Spins on one axis must be learned before spins using two axes

Especially with new jumps, training for the landing should always be given priority over moves in the flight phase. A secure landing is evidenced by even contact over the entire board surface, upright head position facing direction of travel, and cushioning by bending the legs and torso deeply in the transition or landing zone of a jump. This is especially important in training for multiple spins and multiple grabs. If the flight is too short, such actions are inadequate and hurried. That usually leads to an uncontrolled landing.

Further causes of an uncontrolled landing can include:
- Opening the body up too early or too late in a spin
- Inadequate torque at takeoff
- Faulty takeoff timing

That's why freestylers should first work on developing an effective takeoff (see p. 107) and a secure landing, even if it means putting off working on the main phase. At first we recommend fewer spins or grabs, or even simpler variants like straight hits

A secure landing is needed for a good run in the halfpipe.

with no grab. Of course this applies in principle, and doesn't refer just to extremely difficult moves.

With respect to the flight or main phase, the following training goals are a consequence of these considerations:
- Reduction or minimizing movement in the flight phase while learning how to perform a new move
- Gradual increase in height of flight through effective takeoff and controlled increase in approach speed
- Improvement in takeoff timing

When these criteria are sufficiently consistent and landing is secure, then the movements can be developed into the desired figure.

Style

Style occupies, along with additional skills within technique, an increasingly important place in Freestyle training. It allows freestylers to express their creativity. In general, style becomes possible only when these training goals have been reached. It is based on freestylers' individual traits and on their physique, and it is displayed in the following:
- The height and distance of a hit
- Performance of movements in the figure (e.g., extreme twisting of the body and extreme arching in a backside air)
- The number of grab variations
- The speed of the move (e.g., variations in turning speed in spins)
- Harmony and flow of movement
- Creativity in sequencing of various figures
- Personal impression (e.g., aggressive and consistent riding of halfpipe run)

These manifestations of style can be developed through training. You and your friends can make great progress by watching each other. Training together also provides valuable stimulation.

Especially in competition, style should receive a lot of attention.

Equipment Technology

Equipment technology now has a major effect on freestylers' riding technique. This is because of mechanical features and further developments in materials. Board material is matched to the rider in Freestyle according to three important criteria:

▪ The ultimate use of the board
▪ Available tricks and hits
▪ The freestyler's physique

These three criteria influence one another.

Relative to board technology several parameters have emerged as particularly important:

▪ Board length
▪ Board width
▪ Waisting
▪ Board flex
▪ Board weight
▪ Insert systems

In addition, the choice of materials for boots and bindings has expanded. All these factors depend on the three important criteria just listed.

Short boards are well suited for complete spins and are easy to turn, but hard to ride at high speeds. In addition, short boards are harder to handle on high and long straight jumps because they have less gripping area on landing.

Style will become even more important in the future.

On the other hand, longer boards are difficult to "spin"; usually they can spin only up to 540°. The greater board surface proves its worth, however, at high speeds and in high and long, straight hits. But this is at the expense of turning ease. Longer Freestyle boards can also be used very well for freeriding.

Board width is a noticeable factor in turning ease. Wide boards have basically sluggish handling qualities, but are better in deep snow and on landings because of their greater surface and gripping area.

Wider boards also make it possible for riders with big boots to choose an extremely shallow binding angle.

The pronounced waisting of a Freestyle board makes it easier to turn in hits, and it increases overall ease in turning. But in comparison to boards with less waisting, a Freestyle board is harder to handle.

Board flex likewise plays an important role in technique. Softer boards make it easier to do tricks and turns at slower speed.

The flexing of the board is especially evident in takeoffs over the tail or nose. In general, a stiffer board is appropriate to heavier riders.

A stiffer board offers greater stability in approach, takeoff, and landing at higher speeds, or in higher and longer hits. The weight of the board is noticeable especially in hits and turns. Light boards make it easier to initiate turning motions. But they quickly give rise to instability in high and long hits during the flight phase.

Today's insert systems make it possible to choose numerous binding positions. That makes it possible to assume a stance on the board that fits the individual.

We must not neglect to explain board preparation, especially considering the board parameters (see p. 157ff.). A well-prepared Freestyle board improves riding measurably. Board preparation thus becomes an important and valid precondition for successful moves.

To function as a unit,
board and rider should
be well matched.

depend on each rider's physique, body weight, proficiency, conditioning, and riding style. Fortunately, such choices need not be a matter of trial and error. As riders acquire or replace equipment they would be wise to seek the advice of friends and professionals and to consult snowboarding publications and literature available from manufacturers. Ideally, riders might find a way to rent or borrow for a day a piece of equipment that interests them. As moves and the resulting demands that riders place on equipment continue to evolve, there will be a continuous stream of technical refinements long into the future.

Performance Level and Special Technique Training

For special technique training the freestyler's performance level is divided into three ability levels:

- Beginners
- Advanced
- Top-level freestylers

The divisions between the individual performance levels are not clearly defined and will vary among individuals. The following training methods address the three performance levels and are one way to foster a freestyler's technique. In any case, this requires lots of patience and conscientiousness in training.

With respect to safety, the following additional factors must be considered in training on jumps and in halfpipes:

- Jumps should be located in a special training area or at least toward the edge of the trail.
- A second rider should verify that the entire jumping area and especially the landing zone are safe.
- Under no circumstances should anyone else be in the takeoff and landing zones when they are in use.
- Whenever possible, only one person at a time should ride the halfpipe.

Freestyle bindings must hold the heel securely. With additional spins and high or long straight hits, bindings should be very stiff, especially on the heelside edge. This makes it possible to apply strong pressure. Bindings should always be wide enough for the boots. If they are too narrow, they will cause cramps in the legs and feet. Soft bindings with small spoilers are well suited for Freestyle funparks. But in big halfpipes or on big hits they don't provide adequate support.

The boot should provide good support to the foot for transferring force to the board, and it should resist turning.

Freestylers should experiment a lot with all factors. That's the only way they can exhaust the possibilities offered by their board material and advance their own technical potential.

Given the myriad of variations in boot-board-binding combinations, choices of equipment will

Training for Beginners

Training for beginners should be characterized by accumulation of first movement experiences. Here the most important things are safety and caution. The beginner has plenty of possible movement experiences to choose from. In addition, before starting technique training, the beginner should become well informed about the choice of suitable boards.

Beginners can meet the first basic requirement by improving their riding technique. Riding backward and the first basic tricks, such as ollies without grabs, and nose and tail grabs, should be practiced on the slope. For this riding position, central balance is essential. Freeriding essentially contributes to a secure sense of movement at this level.

Low jumps should be used at the beginning. In general, the approach speed and the height and distance of the flight should be quite small. A sufficiently steep landing zone should be chosen for this. The jumps should be flat or only slightly raised. Practice with takeoff and landing is of prime importance in the hits. Takeoff, flight, and landing should be experienced deliberately. Hits consist mostly of straight hits with no grabs.

When some basic movements of these hits are mastered, the first half- or single turns (180° or 360°) along the body's long axis can be performed. For reasons of better orientation and landing safety, it's recommended to learn spin turns in toeside direction before spin turns in heelside direction.

Soon the beginner should start to experiment with higher jumps and with takeoff angles. The first grab variations can be added to hits already learned. Hits can also be carried higher off bigger jumps.

In conjunction with this process the beginner can sample some first experiences in the halfpipe. These should focus at first on riding technique.

Riding from wall to wall should be practiced with different approach angles. The first turning experiences on the jumps are helpful here in direction changes. The distance ridden on the wall should be increased gradually until the coping is reached as a turning point. Turning can be helped by pushing off lightly on the wall-side edge. With adequate visibility, fakie variations can be introduced.

Controlled drop-ins with subsequent riding from wall to wall are basic exercises for beginners.

When these technical maneuvers have been mastered, the first straight hits at moderate approach speed and without grabs can be done. The turning moves toward the transition must not be neglected. The first introduction to inverts can now be included in the program. Appropriate moves include the HoHo Plant Heelside, where the arm support is done with legs drawn up.

Simple heelside airs are among the first hits.

Overall on-snow training should aid in developing a concept of movement by:

- Watching how the first moves are performed by an experienced freestyler
- Experiencing motion in general technique training (e.g., bouncing on trampoline)
- Viewing snowboarding videos that focus on the technical elements under development

Training for Advanced Riders

The advanced rider's goal should be to solidify, refine, and cultivate the moves previously learned and to add them to the repertory. The height of the hits can slowly be increased.

characterized by sequences of hits and tricks. Controlled riding through the flats is very important to turning. Edge pressure should be used in angling through the flats.

The approach position—forward or backward—is varied more and more. Inverts already practiced are done with more pronounced stretches of the entire body, especially the arms, and with the first grabs. Inverts of a higher order of difficulty are first done in a crouch with no grabs. At this ability level the approach speed to hits can be increased gradually. Markings on the wall or the coping, or friends shouting directions, can help with takeoff timing. If a rider encounters problems in coordination such as temporary inability to perform tricks or hits (see p. 67), it is helpful to change to free riding or to a different hit or trick.

Advanced riders gradually increase the height of the jumps they have mastered.

Alley oops belong in the repertory of advanced beginners.

More straight hits and spins around the body's long axis are learned. Spins that have already been learned can be provided with stretch or crouch variations and grabs. Grabs in the turning direction should be done before grabs in the opposite direction. Jumps with a fakie approach can also be developed further.

Spins around the body's long axis (e.g., 360°) which were learned on jumps can be used in the halfpipe. Turns in the toeside direction should be performed before turns in the heelside direction. Grab variations are added to straight hits that have been mastered. Riding the halfpipe is more and more

Freestylers should also not forget to experiment with their board, the binding position, and their boots.

During training riders should watch video clips of their moves and analyze them with friends or the coach. Ineffectual movements and their causes can thus be clearly analyzed and recognized. Likewise, it is helpful to use video clips of tricks and hits to develop style.

Verbal description of overall moves or their component parts and their conscious mental imaging become increasingly important in overall technique training. They provide riders with feedback on their understanding of how the moves work. Riders should stimulate their mental imaging and ideas by watching other riders and snowboarding videos.

Top-level freestylers emphasize refinement of moves, improvement of style, and consistency of movement in competitions.

General on-snow training at this level of development should be complemented by measures for learning and strengthening new moves. This is especially important as riders strive to learn flips.

Turns around the body's broad axis should in any case first be done in accordance with the training possibilities of overall technique training (see p. 103). Doing these moves too soon on jumps or in halfpipes may involve a heightened risk of injury because of increased fear and stress. These stress factors must be avoided at all cost.

The first on-snow flips should be done off a jump. The following parameters are important:

- For back flips, a raised takeoff zone
- Steepness of landing area
- Higher but controlled approach speed

Riders who have mastered the skill of visualizing themselves performing new moves will have a head start. When something new is attempted, riders should be warmed up, fresh, and confident of success. When a new move is begun, much important preparation will already have been done inside the rider's head.

Training for Top-level Freestylers

The main training goal of top-level freestylers is optimal performance and styling of learned hits and tricks under competition conditions. This goal can be reached only when the moves can be executed automatically and consistently, and when they are characterized by excellent timing and increased height of flight.

In the halfpipe numerous complete runs should be done one after another. Freestylers should concentrate intently before each run and go through all the moves once again in their head. It's worthwhile to consider the advantages of training under stress since fatigue distorts movements that demand lots of coordination and leads to training inappropriate movements.

In addition to varied grabs in jumps, which riders may themselves invent, experimenting with complex moves along two turning axes in the halfpipe is part of the training program. These moves presuppose safe and controlled mastery of flips off a jump.

Experimentation must be supported intensively by overall technique training. According to physical abilities, individual development steps can be lengthened based on the greater complexity of movement. This process requires lots of patience. The art of Freestyle lies in perfection of expressiveness in the moves, plus simultaneous performance of new moves. The first should generally be given priority. Further improvement in riding technique can be gained through demanding courses on race training (see p. 48). As they develop, freestylers experiment deliberately with various board materials and develop them further.

Performance of hits and flow of movements should be filmed on video even more intensively than before. In the subsequent analysis of how the moves are performed the criteria depend on goal setting in special technique training (see p. 106). Observation of style in these videos focuses especially on component movements such as hand position in a grab and duration of grab. The difficulty of the hits can't be increased too much at this level.

Organization of Tricks and Hits

This organization provides the freestyler with a first overview. This system should help in choosing hits and tricks. It can be used to select a beginner's first simple figures as well as to organize an entire run in the halfpipe. Due to rapid development this overview is never completely finished. There can always be new figures or adaptations of familiar figures. Especially advanced and top-level freestylers should have the initiative to keep developing this overview.

In the foregoing analysis scheme there is also the possibility of a short preliminary analysis of familiar and new moves. This scheme is based on preexisting thoughts about how to execute moves. It involves the following parameters:
- Category of hit or trick
- Description
- Application
- Axes of turn used in the figure
- Direction of approach (forward or backward)
- Takeoff
- Impetus at takeoff
- Movements during flight phase

- Turn direction (toward heelside, toeside, in direction of nose or tail)
- Arm support phase (inverts)
- Landing or final position
- Style possibilities (dealing only with tips or motivation; riders should always impart their own impression to their style)

An initial system divides figures into major categories:
- Tricks on the slope
- Straight hits
- Inverts
- Spins

Tricks on the slope involve simple figures that can be done in several variations. They are done in the course of riding, without jumps or halfpipe.

Straight hits are hits without turns. But in the halfpipe even these hits involve some small turns along the body's long axis, depending on the approach angle on the wall, in order to get the board set for landing in the transition. Achieving the necessary torque by slightly turning the body is not considered part of the impetus of straight hits in the takeoff.

The board can be oriented forward or backward for landing (airs to fakie). Straight hits can also be described as airs; in the halfpipe, airs are divided into toeside and heelside airs, according to which edge is used for takeoff.

An air jumped on the toeside wall can become a different air on the heelside wall. So, for example, a Slob Air off the toeside wall turns into a Japan Air on the heelside wall.

Airs can also be jumped in alley-oop versions. Here the body makes a clear rotation (usually greater than 180°) upward in the direction of the flat. The requirements for applying torque still apply; just the same, the hits are classified as straight hits or airs.

Figures that involve a brief support phase with one or both arms on the coping of the halfpipe are known as Inverts. In these moves the head is momentarily closer to the halfpipe or to the coping than the board is. Inverts are usually performed in the halfpipe.

Spin tricks are figures that use clear turning movements. They are done off jumps as well as in the halfpipe and are distinguished primarily by:
- Turning axes
- Direction of turn
- Number of turns

The following fact is of great significance relative to the number of turns: Due to landing in the transition when a spin trick is done along the body's long axis, a greater number of turns can be done than with a comparable move off a jump (e.g., a 360°). This also applies to alley-oop versions. The reason lies in the return of the flight path into the transition. Since hits generally consist of 180° segments, a spin jumped and landed in nose direction in the halfpipe contains about 180° more than one done off a jump. This points up the importance of the following in performing these spins in the halfpipe:

- Somewhat longer duration of flight
- Generally faster turns
- Somewhat higher torque prior to takeoff to increase turning impulse during flight

In general there are many possible variations in almost all hits with regard to grabs, direction of approach, turning direction, and landing. So, for example, straight jumps can be done or landed fakie with 180° variations. Alley-oop variations can likewise be done with lots of hits.

Slope Tricks

DESIGNATION: Tail Wheelie

WHERE USED: On slope

DIRECTION OF APPROACH: Forward

MOVEMENT: Weight shift to rear leg with simultaneous lifting of nose with straightened forward leg

END POSITION: Riding straight ahead with upright head position

STYLE POSSIBILITIES: Height of tail wheelies, duration of ride while maintaining wheelie position

DESIGNATION: Lay-back Slide

WHERE USED: On slope, edges, hills, well used halfpipes

DIRECTION OF APPROACH: Forward

MOVEMENT: Deep heelside turn with final body stretch and counterturn of body in direction of tail

SUPPORT PHASE: Support from trailing arm toward backside

END POSITION: Riding on heelside edge with upright head position

STYLE POSSIBILITIES: Pronounced stretching of body and counterturning of body

DESIGNATION: Noseroll 180°

WHERE USED: Slope

TURNING AXIS OF FIGURE: Long axis of body

PRESSURE: Over nose and forward area of heelside edge

MOVEMENT ACCOMPANYING PRESSURE: Weight shift onto forward leg with simultaneous lifting of tail with trailing leg, turning head and torso

TURN DIRECTION: Toward heelside or toeside

STYLE POSSIBILITIES: Lifting tail high, multiple turns on the nose

DESIGNATION: Tailroll 180°

WHERE USED: Slope

TURNING AXIS OF FIGURE: Long axis of body

DIRECTION OF APPROACH: Backward

PRESSURE: Over tail and rear area of heelside edge

MOVEMENT ACCOMPANYING PRESSURE: Weight shift to trailing leg with simultaneous lifting of nose with straightened forward leg and turning of head and torso

DIRECTION OF TURN: Toward toeside or heelside

END POSITION: Riding forward with head and torso turned in direction of travel, upright head position facing direction of travel

STYLE POSSIBILITIES: Pronounced lifting of nose, multiple turns on tail

DESIGNATION: Ollie

WHERE USED: Slope

DIRECTION OF APPROACH: Forward

TAKEOFF: Depending on pitch of slope, either from edge, or in the case of not-too-steep slope, from entire board surface and tail

MOVEMENT AT TAKEOFF: Controlled weight shift to trailing leg with final explosive straightening of legs

MOVEMENTS DURING FLIGHT PHASE: Pulling up legs, grab variations, opening up body on landing

LANDING: Forward; cushioning by bending knees, upright head position facing direction of travel

STYLE POSSIBILITIES: Grab variations, height of hit, 180° turn (fakie) or 360° turn on long axis of body

Straight Hits

DESIGNATION: Slob Air

WHERE USED: Off jumps, in halfpipe

DIRECTION OF APPROACH: Forward

TAKEOFF: Usually from entire board surface (from jump) or toeside edge (toeside wall, halfpipe)

MOVEMENT AT TAKEOFF: Explosive straightening of legs

MOVEMENTS DURING FLIGHT PHASE: Counterturning legs and board relative to torso toward heelside, with simultaneous straightening of rear leg and drawing up of forward leg; grab with front hand on toeside edge, opening of position upon landing

LANDING: Forward. Cushion by bending knees, head held upright

STYLE POSSIBILITIES: Extreme twisting of body upon jumping, holding this position for a long time with sufficient altitude; pronounced stretching of rear leg and bending of front leg; grab variations

---

DESIGNATION: Tailgrab

WHERE USED: Jumps, halfpipe

DIRECTION OF APPROACH: Forward

TAKEOFF: Usually from entire board surface (off jumps) or heelside- or toeside edge (halfpipe)

MOVEMENT UPON TAKEOFF: Explosive straightening of legs

MOVEMENTS DURING FLIGHT PHASE: Extreme pulling up of rear leg and straightening of front leg. Tail grab with rear hand; opening of position in landing

LANDING: Forward; cushioning by bending knees, upright head position facing direction of travel

STYLE POSSIBILITIES: Extreme pulling up of rear leg and straightening of front leg; holding this position for a long time with sufficient altitude; grab variations

---

DESIGNATION: Backside Air

WHERE USED: Jumps, halfpipe

DIRECTION OF APPROACH: Forward

TAKEOFF: Usually from entire board surface (from jumps) or heelside edge (halfpipe)

MOVEMENT AT TAKEOFF: Explosive straightening of legs

MOVEMENTS DURING FLIGHT PHASE: Extreme bending of legs back toward bottom, counterturning head and torso in heelside direction with simultaneous arching of back; grab with forward hand on heelside edge, opening up of position at landing

LANDING: Forward; cushioning by bending knees, upright head position facing direction of travel

STYLE POSSIBILITIES: Extreme counterturning of head and torso and simultaneous extreme arching, holding this position for a long time with sufficient altitude; grab variations

---

DESIGNATION: Japan Air

WHERE USED: Jumps, halfpipe

DIRECTION OF APPROACH: Forward

TAKEOFF: Usually from entire board surface (off jumps) or heelside edge (heelside wall, halfpipe)

MOVEMENT AT TAKEOFF: Explosive straightening of legs

MOVEMENTS DURING FLIGHT PHASE: Counterturning of legs and board relative to torso toward heelside with simultaneous straightening of rear leg and pulling of front leg toward heelside; grab with forward hand on toeside edge, opening position at landing

LANDING: Forward; cushioning by bending knees, upright head position facing direction of travel

STYLE POSSIBILITIES: Extremely pronounced straightening of legs, marked turning of torso in nose direction, maintaining this position for a long time with sufficient altitude; grab variations

---

DESIGNATION: Mute Air

WHERE USED: Jumps, halfpipe

DIRECTION OF APPROACH: Forward

TAKEOFF: Usually from entire board surface (off jumps) or heelside or toeside edge (halfpipe)

MOVEMENT AT TAKEOFF: Explosive straightening of legs

MOVEMENTS DURING FLIGHT PHASE: Pulling in forward leg with simultaneous straightening of rear leg; turning and simultaneous bending of torso toward toeside; grab with forward hand onto toeside edge at level of front binding; opening of position at landing

LANDING: Forward; cushioning by bending knees; upright head position facing direction of travel

STYLE POSSIBILITIES: Extremely pronounced pulling up of front leg with simultaneous straightening of rear leg; pushing hips forward over forward leg, holding this position for a long time with sufficient altitude; grab variations

---

DESIGNATION: Nosegrab

WHERE USED: Jumps, halfpipe

DIRECTION OF APPROACH: Forward

TAKEOFF: Usually from entire board surface (off jumps) or heelside or toeside edge (halfpipe)

MOVEMENT AT TAKEOFF: Explosive straightening of legs

MOVEMENTS DURING FLIGHT PHASE: Pulling up forward leg and straightening rear leg; grab on nose with forward hand and simultaneous pulling nose toward body; opening position at landing

LANDING: Forward; cushioning by bending knees; upright head position facing direction of travel

STYLE POSSIBILITIES: Pronounced pulling up of forward leg, extremely pronounced pulling up on nose toward body; holding this position for a long time with sufficient altitude; grab variations

---

DESIGNATION: Stiffy

WHERE USED: Jumps, halfpipe

DIRECTION OF APPROACH: Forward

TAKEOFF: Usually from entire board surface (off jumps) or heelside or toeside edge (halfpipe)

MOVEMENT AT TAKEOFF: Explosive straightening of legs

MOVEMENTS DURING FLIGHT PHASE: Straightening both legs with simultaneous bending and turning of torso in nose direction; grab by rear hand to toeside edge between bindings; opening position at landing

STYLE POSSIBILITIES: Extremely pronounced straightening of legs, marked turning of torso in nose direction, holding this position for a long time with sufficient altitude; grab variations

---

DESIGNATION: Frontside Air

WHERE USED: Halfpipe

TAKEOFF: From toeside edge (toeside wall, halfpipe)

DIRECTION OF APPROACH: Forward

MOVEMENT AT TAKEOFF: Explosive straightening of legs

MOVEMENTS DURING FLIGHT PHASE: Extreme drawing up of legs; grab with rear hand to toeside edge; opening position at landing

LANDING: Forward, cushioning by bending legs, upright head position facing direction of travel

STYLE POSSIBILITIES: Extreme pulling up of legs, pronounced grab on toeside edge, holding this position for a long time with sufficient altitude, legs as horizontal as possible during flight phase; grab variations

Tailgrab (straight hit)

Frontside air (straight hit)

Nosebone (straight hit)

DESIGNATION: Nosebone

WHERE USED: Halfpipe

TURNING AXIS: Long axis of body in halfpipe

DIRECTION OF APPROACH: Forward

TAKEOFF: Usually from entire board surface (off jumps) or heelside or toeside edge (halfpipe)

MOVEMENT AT TAKEOFF: Explosive straightening of legs

MOVEMENTS DURING FLIGHT PHASE: Pulling up rear leg or straightening front leg; bending torso in nose direction; grab with rear hand on toeside edge; opening position at landing

LANDING: Forward; cushioning by bending knees, upright head position facing direction of travel

STYLE POSSIBILITIES: Extreme pulling up of rear leg or straightening forward leg; pronounced grab on toeside edge; holding this position for a long time with sufficient altitude; legs as horizontal as possible during flight phase; grab variations

DESIGNATION: Method Air

WHERE USED: Halfpipe

DIRECTION OF APPROACH: Forward, with shallow angle of approach

TAKEOFF: From heelside edge (heelside wall)

MOVEMENT AT TAKEOFF: Bending both legs toward bottom with simultaneous arching of body; long axis of body as horizontal as possible; grab with forward hand on backside edge; opening position at landing

LANDING: Forward; cushioning by bending knees, upright head position facing direction of travel

STYLE POSSIBILITIES: Extreme arching, pronounced grab on backside edge, holding this position for a long time with sufficient flight altitude and distance

Nosebone (straight hit)

Method air (straight hit)

Inverts

DESIGNATION: HoHo Plant Backside

WHERE USED: Halfpipe

TURN AXES: Long axis and broad axis of body

DIRECTION OF APPROACH: Forward, with steep approach angle

TAKEOFF: From toeside (toeside wall) or heelside edge (heelside wall)

MOVEMENT AT TAKEOFF: Pronounced turning of head and torso toward transition (with takeoff from heelside wall, toward toeside; with takeoff from toeside wall, toward heelside); just before takeoff, explosive straightening of legs

MOVEMENTS DURING FLIGHT PHASE: Turning of entire body around long and broad axes, straightening of entire body and moving both arms toward coping to set up support

ARM SUPPORT PHASE: Pronounced straightening of arms with pause; ending support phase by bending at hips and pushing off hard from coping; opening of arched position at landing

LANDING: Forward; cushioning by bending knees; upright head position facing direction of travel

STYLE POSSIBILITIES: Pronounced and high leap in support phase, extreme straightening of entire body, adequate lingering in support phase; pronounced push-off from support phase

DESIGNATION: Layback to Fakie

WHERE USED: Halfpipe

TURNING AXES: Long and broad axes of body

DIRECTION OF APPROACH: Forward, with steep approach angle

TAKEOFF: From toeside edge (toeside wall)

MOVEMENT AT TAKEOFF: Pronounced turning of head and body toward transition (toeside) just before takeoff; explosive straightening of legs

MOVEMENTS DURING FLIGHT PHASE: Counterturning torso relative to legs in heelside direction; straightening legs with simultaneous grab by forward hand on heelside edge, moving rear arm toward toeside in direction of coping to set up support

ARM SUPPORT PHASE: Pronounced straightening of rear arm and pause; ending support phase by turning legs toward backside, strong push-off from coping; opening arched position at landing

LANDING: Backward; cushioning by bending knees; upright head position facing direction of travel (head turned toward toeside over rear shoulder)

STYLE POSSIBILITIES: Pronounced, high leap into support phase; extreme straightening of legs, lingering for a while in support phase; pronounced push-off to end support phase

DESIGNATION: Frontside Invert

WHERE USED: Halfpipe

TURNING AXES: Long and broad axes of body

DIRECTION OF APPROACH: Forward, with steep approach angle

TAKEOFF: From toeside edge (toeside wall)

MOVEMENT AT TAKEOFF: Pronounced turning of head and torso toward transition (heelside) just before takeoff; explosive straightening of legs

MOVEMENTS DURING FLIGHT PHASE: Turning of entire body around the long and broad axes of body; straightening legs; movement of forward arm toward heelside in direction of coping

ARM SUPPORT PHASE: Pronounced straightening of arm and pause; bending at hips to end support phase; strong push-off from coping; opening arched position at landing

LANDING: Forward; cushioning by bending knees; upright head position facing direction of travel

STYLE POSSIBILITIES: Pronounced, high leap into support phase; extreme straightening of entire body, lingering a moment in support phase; clear push-off from support phase

DESIGNATION: Andrecht Handplant

WHERE USED: Halfpipe

TURNING AXES: Long and broad axes of body

DIRECTION OF APPROACH: Forward, with steep approach angle

TAKEOFF: From heelside edge (heelside wall)

MOVEMENT AT TAKEOFF: Pronounced turning of head and torso toward transition (toeside) just before takeoff; explosive straightening of legs

MOVEMENTS DURING FLIGHT PHASE: Turning entire body around the long and broad axes, straightening entire body, setup of support with rear arm and simultaneous grab by forward hand to heelside edge

ARM SUPPORT PHASE: Pronounced straightening of support arm, with pause; bending at hips to end support phase; strong push-off from coping; opening arched position at landing

LANDING: Forward; cushioning by bending knees; upright head position facing direction of travel

STYLE POSSIBILITIES: Pronounced, high leap into support phase; extreme straightening of entire body; lingering a moment in support phase; pronounced push-off to end support phase

DESIGNATION: Miller Flip

WHERE USED: Halfpipe

TURNING AXES: Long and broad axes of body

DIRECTION OF APPROACH: Forward, with steep approach angle

TAKEOFF: From toeside edge (toeside wall)

MOVEMENT AT TAKEOFF: Pronounced turning of head and torso toward transition (heelside) just before takeoff; explosive straightening of legs

MOVEMENTS DURING FLIGHT PHASE: Turning entire body around long and broad axes; keeping body bent and legs straight; support by forward arm and simultaneous grab with rear hand on toeside edge

LANDING: Forward; cushioning by bending knees; upright head position facing direction of travel

STYLE POSSIBILITIES: Pronounced, high leap into support phase, extreme straightening of legs, lingering a moment in support phase; pronounced push-off to end support phase

DESIGNATION: Toeside/Heelside Elguerial

WHERE USED: Halfpipe

TURNING AXES: Long and broad axes of body

DIRECTION OF APPROACH: Backward, with steep approach angle

TAKEOFF: From toeside edge (toeside wall) or heelside edge (heelside wall)

MOVEMENT AT TAKEOFF: Pronounced turning of head and torso toward transition and heelside just before takeoff; explosive straightening of legs

MOVEMENTS DURING FLIGHT PHASE: Turning entire body around long and broad axes in heelside direction; straightening entire body and moving trailing arm toward heelside and coping

ARM SUPPORT PHASE: Pronounced straightening of support arm and pause; turning legs toward toeside with simultaneous holding of torso in support phase; pulling legs up with simultaneous grab with forward hand to heelside edge; bending at hips to end support phase while retaining grab; strong push-off from coping; opening arched position at landing

LANDING: Forward; cushioning by bending at knees, upright head position facing direction of travel

STYLE POSSIBILITIES: Pronounced, high leap into support phase; extreme straightening of legs, pronounced turning of legs in support phase, lingering a moment in support phase; pronounced push-off to end support phase

Miller flip (invert)

Toeside/heelside elguerial (invert)

Spin Tricks

DESIGNATION: Spin tricks around the body's long axis, e.g., 360°, 540°, and 720°

WHERE USED: Jumps, halfpipe

TURN AXIS: Long axis of body

DIRECTION OF APPROACH: Forward or backward

TAKEOFF: From as much of board surface as possible (off jumps) or from toeside or heelside edge (halfpipe)

MOVEMENT AT TAKEOFF: Pronounced turning of head and torso in chosen turn direction just before takeoff; explosive straightening of legs

MOVEMENTS DURING FLIGHT PHASE: Maintaining turning of head and torso as long as possible; variations in body posture (upright, bent toward toeside or nose; arching with grab on heelside edge); variations in position of legs (pulling up both legs, pulling up forward leg); grab variations (toeside, heelside, nose); opening body at landing

LANDING: Forward or backward; cushioning by bending knees; upright head position facing direction of travel

STYLE POSSIBILITIES: Holding a grab for a long time with adequate flight altitude and distance; variations in turning speed; numerous grab variations

DESIGNATION: McTwist (heelside)

WHERE USED: Halfpipe

TURNING AXES: Long and broad axes of body

DIRECTION OF APPROACH: Forward

TAKEOFF: From heelside edge and tail with as-steep-as-possible approach angle

MOVEMENT AT TAKEOFF: Strong turning of head and torso over toeside with simultaneous bending of torso toward tail just before takeoff; explosive straightening of legs

MOVEMENTS DURING FLIGHT PHASE: Further turning of head and torso with simultaneous pronounced bending of torso toward tail; turning legs in toeside direction and simultaneous movement of forward arm to grab toeside edge in front of forward binding; turning around diagonal axis of body is done parallel to coping with simultaneous continuation of turn around body's long axis (the board turns farther toward the toeside) until board is headed toward transition; opening body and releasing grab upon landing in transition

LANDING: Forward; cushioning by bending knees, upright head position facing direction of travel

STYLE POSSIBILITIES: Height, holding grabs for a long time, different body positions in turns (straight, crouching), numerous grab variations

DESIGNATION: Hakon Flip

WHERE USED: Halfpipe

TURNING AXIS: Broad axis of body

DIRECTION OF APPROACH: Backward, fakie

TAKEOFF: From toeside edge on heelside wall

MOVEMENT AT TAKEOFF: Strong arching of torso toward heelside with simultaneous stretching head upward just before takeoff; explosive straightening of legs

MOVEMENTS DURING FLIGHT PHASE: Further reaching with head toward heelside and maintaining arch in torso; pulling up legs during turn toward heelside; moving trailing arm to grab toeside or heelside edge between bindings; turning around the body's diagonal axis perpendicular to the coping; sighting on landing zone in transition during turns around body's diagonal axis; opening body; releasing grab and directing board toward transition for landing

LANDING: Forward; cushioning by bending knees; upright head position facing direction of travel

STYLE POSSIBILITIES: Altitude, holding grabs, different body posture in turns (straight, crouching), numerous grab variations

Spin trick around body's long axis

McTwist heelside (spin trick)

Hakon flip (spin trick)

Preparation for Competition

The general development and increasingly tight competitive fields in Freestyle make deliberate preparation more important than ever. This pertains to organization of overall training for an important competition as well as to long-term and immediate psychological preparation.

Riders' technical performance levels will become even more compacted in the near future. Freestylers' ability to concentrate will then become a more important performance factor than ever. The ability to concentrate has multifaceted influences, and they affect different riders in different ways. They manifest themselves in the familiar "prestart jitters" as well as in the anxiety threshold following injury.

Coping with these psychological stresses is crucial in Freestyle. Some riders turn to conversation and fun for distraction, while others are more reserved. This of course depends greatly on the personality of the riders.

Even at top levels of Freestyle, riders have developed individual tactics and rituals to deal with "prestart jitters." Generally they include overall warm-ups and practice runs, plus some other measures. But often this systematic tuning to a high point in performance is lacking, or is easily disturbed.

The goal of freestylers should be to create conditions that allow successful completion of a competition or a very difficult move under the most relaxed conditions possible. One way to create these conditions and to encourage performance is through deliberate psychological training.

The basic requirement for this step is the rider's own readiness, conviction, and insight into this training, which without those qualities will lose its effectiveness.

Possible types of training have already been touched upon (see p.70) and can be transferred to Freestyle without difficulty. The descriptions given there are useful at the entry level. This is, however, no universal prescription. Freestylers are capable of evaluating themselves through these training possibilities and dealing with any problems that arise, such as anxiety.

Anyone who decides to undertake such training should take it as guidance and integrate it into the overall training program. The key with this is regularity.

Technique training plays an important role in regard to the freestyleer's psyche. Psychological strength develops further only when it deals with measured stresses in training (e.g., with special jumps that a rider avoids) and in competition. Riders who continually demand too little of themselves can be happy with this condition only if their performance expectations are correspondingly low. This is no sure way to achieve success even if it seems within reach. Emotional elements such as nervousness and anxiety, which were mentioned earlier, are also factors in the special development of the psyche. Their continued presence in training and competition leads to stagnation in performance. They can be eliminated in various ways (see p.73).

The possibilities and the effectiveness of psychological training methods have been adequately demonstrated. Freestylers who have not yet developed tactics involving this increasingly important difficulty, or who have had doubts about it, should resolve to implement these training methods. This applies to top-level freestylers as well as for beginners.

Careful supervision by a coach is always important even in Freestyle.

Ability to concentrate, willpower, and determination are important factors in success.

Free riding

In the last few years a discipline has emerged that has opened up new dimensions: Freeriding. Anyone who has experienced this exciting form of snowboarding remains under its spell. A while ago Freeriding was practically inaccessible to normal snowboarders. It has recently been made popular by many of the world's best riders, such as Craig Kelly. The freedom and lightness in powder have been featured in many videos and magazines. But is this dream becoming a reality ?

Snowboarding has many faces;

in Freeriding it's especially important

to know where this sport came from.

Behind it are snowboarding's roots.

When lifts and trails were still taboo for American snowboarders, the order of the day was hiking into the mountains. The motivation for the climb was the ride through undisturbed terrain. Hiking became an important activity for a hard-core fringe group who called themselves snowboarders. From the symbiosis of hiking and "soul-surfing" there arose in the early stages of snowboarding a view of life, a philosophy. For people who seek the ultimate Freeriding adventure, the two areas are practically inseparable. They have a fascination that's unique to snowboarding.

A preparatory stage to Freeriding as understood here involves riding various types of slopes. Mostly that entails going up in cable cars and on lifts. This is simpler and more comfortable; but if you want the absolute "soul kick" you have to get away from the hassle on the slopes.

Freeriding signifies meditation in the alpine winter world. In the search for something new snowboarders experience an indescribable and unique sense of movement. Earlier we had no access to lifts and trails; today it's the impetus toward a different experience that leads us back to the roots of snowboarding.

Back to the roots:
Hiking into snowboarding's
primitive times allows
its rebirth.

BASICS

Freeriding has been marketed aggressively in recent years. Lots of images have been created and the target group of snowboarders have been showered with them. Unthinking imitation has dreadful, even fatal results. Many mountaineering and nature clubs have come to view snowboarders as the epitome of the "alpine apocalypse."

It should be noted that the present chapter has nothing to do with the images that have stamped the discipline with commercialism.

People who undertake Freeriding experience in an impressive way the relationship between nature and humans. Body movements and means of locomotion adapt to nature. They dovetail into the terrain by forming trails, and they remain in our memory as a unique experience.

Any freerider who fails to understand that nature is the stronger may sooner or later fall by the wayside. This is the price for the incomparable experience of Freeriding. It's still worth it.

Freeriding is a challenge, and for every snowboarder it means treading new ground. Added to the rules of conduct on the slope are the laws of nature that stamp the behavior of the freerider. Observing nature and the environment are of course foremost among them. Other fundamentals that determine a freerider's conduct include a willingness to accept risk, strong self-confidence, and a readiness to turn back while on a tour. A realistic self-evaluation of personality and athletic ability complete this behavior. Misjudgments must be avoided at all costs. Anybody who ignores all these points will not come down off the trail. Every rider must continually check that the basic philosophy of Freeriding remains clear. It develops through further experience and empowers the freerider with the ability to adapt conduct to different situations. This is the only way that a snowboarder should go into undisturbed nature.

Freeriding signifies limitless experience of nature, but not at the expense of nature.

Modest risk acceptance _____

Willingness to cancel a tour and turn back _____

Objective evaluation of individual athletic ability _____

Experience

Experience is the guarantee of safety and should be basic to every freerider. Experience should be accumulated with foresight and deliberation; above all else, it requires time. Anyone who opts for Freeriding should consult an expert who can provide important safety tips for beginners and help them acquire experience in undeveloped terrain. An expert can make the ascent easier and prevent beginners from attempting to go on a tour alone.

Accumulating experience should be seen by the freerider as an important part of developing in the discipline. If you want to gain more experience you should do so under the guidance of an expert in back country. The following are some important considerations:

- Assessment of the local flora and fauna in the winter
- Appropriate actions in case of accident
- Evaluation of snow and weather conditions
- Assessment of terrain
- Adjustment of riding technique to conditions
- Handling of equipment

Basic Philosophy of Freeriders:

Readiness to increase awareness of nature and environment _____

Heightened safety consciousness _____

EQUIPMENT FOR THE FREERIDER

Just like the other disciplines in snowboarding, Freeriding places the highest demands on equipment. But here there is a further difference from conventional snowboarding, since the equipment is different in many regards.

Equipment for Freeriding can be divided into three areas. First is the minimal equipment required for safety. Second and third are the basic and special equipment that is necessary for any given tour. Owning and bringing along this equipment does not provide the necessary safety. Only expert familiarity with it will bring quick help and rescue in an emergency. Every piece of equipment that needs explanation is designated with the letter *E* in the freerider's equipment checklist (see p.137). The checklist also clarifies the priorities of individual pieces of equipment: very important equipment not to be left behind is designated with a red square. Items whose usefulness depends on the tour or its duration are designated with a blue square.

Minimum Equipment Required for Safety

There is no way a freerider can do without safety equipment. Ignorance endangers one's own life and that of others. Safety items include transceivers known as avalanche beacons (AB) for people buried in slides, an avalanche shovel, an avalanche probe, a bivouac sac or space blanket, and a first-aid kit. Every one of these items must be brought along in case they are needed to save a life. All items complement one another and can be used sensibly only in combination with the others. Immediate search and rescue by remaining participants is practically the only hope for survival in the case of an avalanche.

Merely bringing along the minimal safety equipment doesn't save your life or anyone else's, though. Learning how to use the equipment is a basic requirement before the first Freeriding trip. The training should always take place under expert supervision. Mountaineering clubs or schools offer extensive training in equipment use.

All members of a Freeriding party should consider themselves as members of a team. Their skills and the equipment they carry complement each other, and all would be needed in case of an emergency. Teamwork means staying in contact with one another while climbing and riding, and knowing how to use the equipment for which each rider is responsible whenever it's needed. Such proficiency and mutual reliance might one day be needed to save a life.

In addition to bringing along an activated AB device, riders should practice regularly with the avalanche beacon and other essential equipment. Of all the equipment, the avalanche beacon is especially deserving of emphasis.

Avalanche Beacon (AB)

The AB is the heart of safety equipment. This device is a combination electronic sender and receiver. The DIN- and CE-tested single-frequency or double-frequency device should always be used. Manufacturers offer fine devices with battery level indicators, optical search indicators, clear speaker signals, long effective range, and automatic on-switch. The device should be fool-proof. Other important points a freerider should look for in an AB are how it's attached to the body, and a casing designed to avoid interfering with movement.

Avalanche beacons make it possible to find someone quickly who has been buried, as long as:

■ All participants are carrying a compatible device on their body.
■ A functional check is performed before each tour.
■ The devices are set to *send* at the start of the tour.
■ Participants have practiced with the devices, especially how to conduct a search.
■ Every participant has an avalanche shovel.

The negligence of freeriders who have never tested all the functions of their AB at home can endanger their lives and those of their comrades. Further important information can be obtained from the owner's manual of these devices or from experts. Additionally, courses on avalanches are recommended to learn how to use the AB safely. New supplements to the AB include the ABS Avalanche Airbag System, available on the market for several years now; it is designed to keep the user from sinking into a mass of moving snow in an avalanche. But on longer tours the heavier weight of this system should be considered.

Avalanche Shovels

An avalanche shovel belongs with every AB; without it a person who's been buried cannot be located quickly. Aside from this most important function, the avalanche shovel has some others: it's useful in assessing snow conditions, and it can be used to save someone from sliding out of control. Furthermore it's a help to freeriders who need to create flat spots in order to buckle into their bindings in steep terrain. Additionally, the avalanche shovel can be used to build an igloo, and a good multifunctional avalanche shovel can also be used as an ax, a snow anchor, and part of an emergency sled. The avalanche shovel should be lightweight and take up a minimum amount of space. The handle should be adjustable for right- and left-handed people. The shaft should be made of strong, light metal such as aluminum, and should be adjustable for length. The blade should be as large as possible and made of durable material stiff enough to resist warping. Resistance to chipping is also important in very cold weather.

Avalanche Probe

An avalanche probe is a mechanical system that aids in precise locating when used in conjunction with an AB. In addition, this device can be used for checking snow cover, sounding crevasses, or determining snow depth. The probe should be very light but supple and shockproof. With a quick assembly system it can be put together fast and stored easily in a pack when taken apart. A three-color scheme makes it easier to determine snow depth. The tip of the probe should be thicker than its diameter so the probe can easily be pulled back out of the snow.

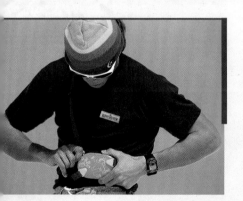

Bivouac Sack and First-aid Equipment

The bivouac sack, an extremely light emergency tent, has a place in every backpack. In bivouacking it is an essential element of protection against storm, rain, and snow. In case of accident it can be used to protect against the cold and aid in transporting an injured person. It should be large enough for two people, and it should have two ventilation or arms slits. It should be provided with enough loops so it can be stowed easily.

The first-aid kit also has its place in the backpack. Complete kits are available from several companies.

Basic Equipment for Freeriders

Getting together the freerider's equipment is done with a view to how it will be used and its weight. These two points pertain to climbing aids, carrying systems, and the board-boot-binding system. Equipment included takes into account the length of the tour and the nature of the terrain. One can choose short trips that last only a few hours, or trips that last one or more days. Choice of equipment is determined by steepness of terrain and expected snow conditions.

Weight is of great importance in Freeriding. It is a permanent limiting factor and should always be carefully considered in gathering equipment. The following observations contribute to sensible equipment choices.

Climbing Aids

The first time you get away from the hassles of lifts with your board and penetrate the alpine winter world, you often wish for the luxury of the slopes. Freeriding is different in many ways. The most basic difference from conventional snowboarding is the lack of cable cars and lifts to carry us to the highest peaks.

A special form of Freeriding is helicopter snowboarding. This is a luxury version of Freeriding that's available only to a minority of riders with very deep pockets, and that raises some ecological questions. The following tips and information are useful even in helicopter snowboarding:

For hundreds of years people have been wracking their brains over a good way to get around in snow. In essence, the results have been snow shoes, skis (in whatever form), and of course, in our time, the snowboard.

Freeriding requires another means of travel because of the climb and long flat areas encountered in touring. This has additional consequences: the weight of the equipment keeps going up, except in the case of a split snowboard. The circumstances of changing the means of travel must be carefully considered. And you should remember to use telescoping poles in climbing and on flat sections.

A beginner who has become familiar with these conditions has no further obstacles to enjoying Freeriding.

Climbing aids for snowboarders have been around for some time now. Occasionally manufacturers have addressed these needs. To date there have been three different possible climbing aids: snow shoes, touring snowboards that can be converted into two skis, and short skis that can be put together. Each system has special advantages and disadvantages. Before we go into each system in detail, a couple of basic observations are in order. The following factors, which have already been explained a couple of times, have an effect on how climbing aids are used.

At the start of a Freeriding trip you have to climb up using your own muscle power.

Weather Conditions and Terrain:
Weather conditions and terrain are the toughest factors to evaluate for use of climbing aids and must always be considered carefully in the preliminary stages of a tour. These factors point out the limitations of any climbing aids. Because of these limitations, in extreme cases freeriders may have to abandon a tour and turn back.

Length of Tour:
As already mentioned, the length of a tour influences the weight of the equipment. There is an essential difference between short trips lasting a few hours and a tour of several days. The longer the tour, the more important economy of movement in climbing becomes. The degree of fatigue is heavily dependent on climbing technique and therefore on climbing aids.

Weight of Equipment:
Equipment weight is an important consideration in Freeriding. It can greatly influence the rider's performance on a tour. It can also have an effect on riding technique. The goals should be to reduce weight as much as possible. This must be considered in the light of the tour length, the terrain, the additional equipment required, and the accompanying increase in weight.

Athletic Ability:
Athletic ability (see p.12) is influenced by all the factors just mentioned. Technique and economy of movement with any climbing aids are directly dependent on athletic ability.

Snowshoes

Snowshoes are the oldest means people have for getting around in snow. Even freeriders have discovered snowshoes for their purposes. They are especially suited to riders who use soft boots. The snowboard must be carried on the backpack. The soft boot is secured to a movable part of the binding by means of thongs. The pivoting of this part allow the foot optimal freedom of movement in walking. Handling still takes some getting used to, but is possible even with gloves on.

Snowshoe frames should be of strong material such as aluminum, and the mesh of cold-resistant rubber or plastic. Snowshoes are available in different sizes according to body size and weight.

Iron points (or "bear claws") in the area of the binding are essential for frozen snow. They go at the ball of the foot or around the entire edge of the foot and continue behind the movable part of the binding. They must be long enough and made so that they don't fill up with ice. Snowshoes with inadequate points that fill with ice are a drain on energy during a climb, and they can lead to complete physical

On shorter Freeriding trips showshoes can be used because of their relatively light weight. Walking on snowshoes requires lifting the feet rather high because of the absence of glide in forward motion.

exhaustion and scuttling a tour. In contrast to touring skis, snowshoes use no energy-saving glide in forward motion. Continually lifting the feet produces rapid muscular fatigue.

Riders who elect to use snowshoes should develop an efficient and economical stride and be in good overall condition. Usually snowshoes are best suited for short tours in deep snow. This climbing method quickly reaches its limitations in steep, frozen, or icy terrain. Its major advantage is its relatively light weight.

Split Snowboards

A few years ago a manufacturer brought out the first split snowboards. These can be taken apart lengthwise and can be converted in just a couple of steps into a pair of skis for the climb. Riders who use this system have to use hard boots and bindings, for boards are available only in this combination. For conversion the plate bindings are unbolted and turned in the direction of travel. By turning the binding and unbolting points on nose and tail (Nitro System), the board comes apart. The bindings, which now lie in the direction of travel, have a good pivot point at the forward edge of the binding. This permits conventional movement as with a touring ski.

During the ascent, climbing skins are put on, as with touring skis. The binding can be fitted with points. Because the skis are so short they should always be used with points. The binding is no safety binding. However, it can be converted from travel mode by bolting it into a fixed position for short runs. In that configuration the skis should be restricted to the short run. Otherwise the skis are reassembled as a snowboard by reattaching at the four points.

The advantage of the system is that it involves no additional weight and that it's comfortable to use. This means it's less of an energy drain during the ascent and on flat sections. Freeriding beginners should pay particular attention to this point. The system is also well adapted for longer tours.

The lengthwise separation of the snowboard may, however, have a major impact on its handling properties in many situations. Soft boot freaks and experienced freeriders who get their kicks only on a Freeriding board with soft bindings won't find this system too appealing.

The comfort of touring skis is approached through the use of climbing skins and points. The takedown snowboard makes ascent and descent easier for the climber thanks to reduced weight. But there may be some compromises in handling qualities.

"Hiker" System Takedown Short Skis

The "Hiker" takedown short ski is the newest development among climbing aids for freeriders. The heart of this construction is the bolting mechanism for the two ski halves. When assembled, the ski has an adequate length of about 55 inches (140 centimeters). Taken apart, the two parts of a ski are just half that length. They can be carried inside or on the outside of the backpack.

The ski can used for climbing by either soft boot or hard boot riders. By changing the mounting, riders can reconfigure the "Hiker" system from one to the other with their own hands. The binding has a climbing aid and can be fitted with points if the going gets icy. Points should always be used because the skis are so short. Climbing skins are also used for the ascent. Because of the way the bindings are made, the energy-efficient movement of the touring ski is achieved in climbing. For major runs the walking mechanism can be bolted down. This system likewise does not constitute a safety binding. The "Hiker" necessitates transporting the snowboard on the backpack. The system's many possibilities demonstrate how many ways it can be used. It's the only climbing system that offers all possibilities in choice of snowboard and boots. The "Hikers" handle reliably in extreme terrain. They involve a little extra weight. Anyone who would like to discover Freeriding, however, should find them acceptable.

Takedown skis allow
use of soft or hard boots.

Climbing Skins

Climbing skins are necessary for both systems of split touring snowboards and "Hiker" short skis. Good quality material is absolutely necessary. The climbing skins stay on by means of a special adhesive on the running surface of the skis and are attached at the tails and tips of the skis. Attachment at the tips is usually by means of a rubber band. The rubber must be very durable and resistant to cold so it doesn't break.

The width of the climbing skins should not quite cover the steel edges at the narrowest part of the waist. When the skins are taken off they are stuck to one another by the running surface. That way no snow can stick to the adhesive side. The adhesive surface must be kept dry and free of snow especially when it's cold out. The adhesive surfaces should generally be kept clean. After a tour the climbing skins should be hung up to dry with the adhesive surfaces together.

Dismantling the takedown ski in
the middle and taking off the skin.

Telescoping Ski Poles

Freeriders can use telescoping ski poles for climbing and in flat areas. They help in maintaining balance and in moving forward. The highest demands are placed on these pieces of equipment. In choosing telescoping ski poles you should pay close attention to stability and weight. The grips should be ergonomically shaped and the grip straps should have plenty of adjustment. The length can be set according to a scale on the shafts. In the photo below you can see both the locking rings and the scale on the lower part of the pole shaft. The threaded locking rings should work smoothly and be immune to icing up; pole tips must be replaceable and made of hardened steel.

Crampons

Crampons should be fitted to the boots before the start of the tour. Normally they don't fit the sole of the boot perfectly. With hard boots crampons can be provided with crampon bindings and may be adjustable for width. For soft boot riders there is a compromise in the form of a crampon with straps. This system doesn't have as much hold, but it's the only possibility for soft boots.

Telescoping ski poles are useful climbing aids; they should be lightweight but strong because they are often leaned on in steep terrain.

Freeriders should use twelve-point crampons. The crampons should be adjusted so that the front points stick out beyond the front of the boot.

Carrying Systems

Backpacks are mandatory for Freeriding. The construction and capacity of the pack depend on the length of the tour. As already explained in the section on Minimal Safety Equipment, there must be a place reserved in the carrying system for an avalanche shovel, an avalanche probe, a bivouac sack, and a first-aid kit. Devices for attaching the board differ according to make. The snowboard must be secured to the pack to keep it from falling to either side. In any case the board is attached to the outside of the pack. On each side of the pack, according to its size, two or three straps are useful for carrying the climbing aids and the telescoping poles. An additional pocket on the top flap is necessary for small tools and snacks. The shoulder and chest straps should be wide enough and well cushioned. A chest strap should link the shoulder straps for descent. The carrying system should fit the back properly and be well padded.

For short Freeriding trips a pack capacity of about 1,800 cubic inches (twenty liters) is adequate. With many brands of these small-volume packs access to the interior is possible from the carrying side. On tours of several days' duration backpacks with a capacity of 3,600 cubic inches (40 liters) or more should be used. The weight of these packs plays a major role with respect to the accumulated weight of the equipment. Due to the weight of the equipment you should pay particular attention to the padding in the areas just mentioned, and if need be, a good anatomic fit (changeable shape and adjustment).

There is no shortage of sources for good carrying systems. Even if local shops have little to offer, there are plenty of catalogs available from suppliers and buying cooperatives. Many of these advertise in periodicals devoted to snowboarding, mountaineering, and camping. It's useful to try on a pack and frame before purchasing, whenever possible, in order to assure proper fit. Remember that the clothing you wear on a trek into the back country and the equipment you carry may make your pack feel different from when you try it on in a shop. As with all types of equipment, you should buy the best you can afford. Your pack will be subjected to great demands, and you will always appreciate quality when you are miles away from repair facilities and your well being depends on the reliability of your equipment.

Hard boots and plate bindings have some advantages because of the better transfer of force to the board. Climbing on foot and the use of crampons are less troublesome because of the hard sole. But the classic Freeriding feeling in powder is not as easy to achieve with this boot-binding system. With any boots it's important to get the best possible fit. Especially in climbing, an improper fit can produce blisters on the heels.

Especially on longer tours a backpack should fit well and be provided with comfortable carrying straps.

Snowboard—Bindings—Boots

The combination of board, bindings, and boots depends on the preference of the rider for one system or the other and on how they will be used. The unique experience of riding in powder is completed by the feeling you get from riding the board. This is characterized by the greatest possible freedom in the ankles. The key to that is the use of soft boots and soft bindings. But soft boots and bindings have drawbacks, too. Those become evident in extremely steep and icy terrain, especially in climbing on foot on excessively steep, icy slopes (over 40°). Use of crampons on soft boots (see Crampons) is not without problems. Only strap-on crampons can be used, and they must fit precisely.

Soft boots and bindings also jostle in descents in steep, icy terrain because of the delayed transfer of force to the edge of the board. Only very good riders master the system under such conditions.

Board Material

In general, wider boards are used in Freeriding. They perform better in deep snow. In addition, these boards are often longer and therefore have a greater bearing surface, and that contributes to greater riding fun. The choice of a board depends greatly on the rider's individual requirements and on how it will be used. The connections between riding technique and board material, which have already been explained for racing and Freestyle (see pp. 65ff. and 111ff., respectively), also come into play here.

Wider boards are often used in Freeriding.

Clothing

Clothing used in Freeriding is often subjected to greater stress than that used on trails. The distinctive stresses in climbing and descending place different demands on clothing.

Underwear

The body warms up a lot during a climb. Often people strip their upper bodies down to underwear even in cold temperatures. On the other hand, it's usually cold in the descent because of the wind from riding or weather conditions. In any case the freerider should wear good-quality underwear.

Formerly, manufacturers had recourse to natural wool. A scientific experiment demonstrated lower energy expenditure while wearing wool underwear rather than conventional materials, given the same physical demands. In addition, this natural material breathes well and allows body sweat to escape to the outside. Another advantage of this material is that in contrast to other materials it remains odorless even when it's worn for a long time. This material can easily be worn even on sensitive skin. People who can think of nothing but a scratchy wool sweater can choose conventional materials.

Depending on the tour, one or two short-sleeved undershirts and possibly a long-sleeved undershirt, plus one or two pairs of long underwear should be brought along. Let's mention the socks here too. Anyone who's underway for a long time will appreciate good socks. Freeriding is hard on socks and they should always be reinforced in the heel. Good warm socks should be used according to the weather.

Outerwear

As already mentioned, clothing is subjected to lots of stress. Design must correspond to function. Tops and pants should be made of strong materials. The fabric should have a breathable membrane and be water resistant. Good fleece fabric is standard for sweaters.

A vest that can be carried in the jacket makes sense. Pants and jacket should have a number of good-size pockets. They can even hold a map.

The jacket must close tightly at top and bottom in powder and bad weather conditions. Pants cuffs should have a closure for use in deep snow.

Gloves

Depending on the tour, a freerider will need one or two pairs of gloves. Wool gloves are good for climbing. They are very durable and they afford ample freedom of movement.

For the descent a good pair of snowboarding gloves with removable liners and cuffs long enough for deep snow should be used. Depending on weather conditions this can be a glove or a mitten. To save weight, you could leave the glove liners home and use the wool gloves with the shells. You should try this at home before starting the tour.

Important Accessories

The following small items should always be brought along on a tour. A cap protects against UV rays and cold when it snows. It can be complemented by a storm hood. In very warm weather baseball caps and headbands are useful.

Sunglasses and ski goggles are very important. They should provide absolute protection against UV rays. Sunglasses should let no light in from the sides. At this point we should also mention sun screen and lip balm, which must never be forgotten.

Freeriders' clothing is subjected to lots of wear and tear.

Blister patches can be extremely helpful. They have saved many tours from being terminated prematurely. You should always bring along enough provisions and a drink in a thermos or a water bottle. A small tool kit with necessary replacement parts can provide insurance against unpleasant surprises.

An experienced freerider who goes on a group tour without an official guide should bring a map, a compass, and a watch with an integral altimeter. The rider must also have a thorough understanding of how to use this equipment.

Special Equipment

Special equipment involves gear that's necessary on specific tours based on terrain conditions or the type of tour. Glacier equipment is an example. It's absolutely essential on a glacier tour. Most of that equipment needs some explanation. That ranges from putting on crampons to techniques for locating someone who's fallen into a crevasse.

On long tours a headlamp and maybe a sleeping bag with a foam pad and washing implements are important. In the spring hiking trails are often free of snow. Recently mountain bikes have been used to get up to snow level. A mountain bike is a very welcome aid, especially on the return trip. Its use necessitates return to the same point of departure, though.

Freeriders' Equipment Checklist

Minimal Equipment Required for Safety:

Bivouac sack _____

First-aid kit (E) _____

Avalanche shovel _____

Avalanche probe (E) _____

Avalanche beacon (AB) (E) _____

Basic Equipment:
Climbing Aids:
- Snowshoes
- Split touring snowboard with climbing skins and ice points
- Takedown short "Hiker" skis with climbing skins and ice points
- Possibly crampons for soft boots
- Telescoping ski poles

Board-Boot Systems:
- Soft boots—snowboard with shell bindings
- Snowboard—hard boots—Snowboard or takedown touring snowboard with plate bindings
- Backpack with carrying arrangement for snowboard (capacity dependent upon tour)

High-performance Clothing:
- Fleece pullover
- High-performance underwear, socks (extra-high quality, according to tour)
- Outer clothing for snowboarding (jacket, pants)
- Cap and headband
- Storm hood
- Snowboarding gloves, plus a thinner pair of gloves for the climb

Important Accessories:
- Sunglasses and ski goggles with total UV protection
- Sunscreen and lip balm
- Blister patches
- Food
- Thermos with warm drink or water bottle
- Compact tool kit with most important replacement parts
- Watch with altimeter (E)
- Maps (E)
- Compass (E)

Special Equipment:
Glacier Equipment:
- Ropes (chest belt, hip belt, and sling) (E)
- Ice ax (E)
- Carabiners (E)
- Prusick slings (E)
- Rope (E)
- Crampons (E)
- Mountain bike (for long trips in spring)
- Head lamp
- Sleeping bag, foam pad
- Washing implements

E = Experience/explanation needed with these items of equipment

STRESS PROFILE OF FREERIDERS

Athletic ability is not the limiting factor only in racing or in the halfpipe. It's also a basic part of how freeriders meet their challenges. The complexity of the factors that influence athletic ability also applies to Freeriding.

Conditioning

Freeriding can basically be divided into two distinct stress phases. The first phase includes climbing and moving through flat sections of terrain. The second phase consists of the descent with the snowboard. They alternate according to terrain. There is an additional physical strain on the snowboarder in Phase I that must be dealt with.

The weight of the equipment plays a major role on every tour. It presents additional physical strain in both phases.

An exception to this is riding in areas close to maintained slopes. There the strain of climbing is reduced or eliminated because of the presence of cable cars or lifts.

Adapting technique to situation at hand is very important in undeveloped terrain.

138

The limiting factors in conditioning are strength and endurance. Muscle work in climbing and crossing flat sections is added to the muscle strain of riding the board. Greater demands are placed on the shoulder and back muscles because of the backpack and because of the use of ski poles. Also, the higher you climb, the thinner the oxygen is, and that's a limiting factor as well. For these reasons, freeriders should intentionally improve their conditioning during the off-season.

Tactics

It's possible to speak of certain tactics even in Freeriding. That constitutes part of the fascination for Freeriding. This is not a question of tactics against a potential opponent, but rather the rider's physical tactics, such as conserving energy or adapting ability and experience to different situations throughout the tour.

Framework

The decisive factor for a successful Freeriding adventure is the overarching situational framework. External conditions are dictated by weather, terrain, and equipment. In extreme cases they can cause cancellation of the tour. Endogenous (inner) conditions such as health or time pressure can also have a major limiting effect.

Technique

Good technique is the key to the unique motion experience of Freeriding. Riders who work on their coordination and their moves before the season discover in this snowboarding discipline practically endless possibilities for physical variety and creativity (see Riding Style and Technique).

Personality Traits

Personality traits likewise have a great influence on the stress profile of freeriders. They involve the rider's physical and psychological demands. Knowing these traits and the objective self-evaluation already mentioned are important parts of planning for a tour. They contribute measurably to risk reduction.

Physical Preparation

Freeriders' physical preparation should begin in the summer. Personal standards, expectations for the coming season, and the freerider's stress profile are critical in preparing for the season. Riders who expect a lot from the winter have to invest more time in training. Training should be continually evaluated.

Training for conditioning should be varied and ongoing. Training is done in accordance with available time. Three hours per week is an absolute minimum. At the start, the basic requirement is building up fundamental endurance. Pulse rate should fall between 120 and 140 beats per minute for this purpose. Mountain biking, in-line skating, jogging, and swimming are good choices for this conditioning.

The scope of training should increase over the course of several weeks before the intensity of the training is increased. Heart rate can then go up to between 140 and 160 beats per minute. Intensive agility training should be conducted parallel to this program. Training with a mountain bike or with in-line skates also offers an opportunity to improve coordination. Single tracks, trails, and downhills offer fine possibilities for mountain biking. And there are specially constructed parks for in-line skating.

Training is continually expanded in scope and intensity until the fall. Maximum heart rate should be a regular part of training. Long uphills on the mountain bike, lengthy mountain runs, or rollerblading in hilly terrain are now part of the program. Once again, agility must not be neglected. Snowboarding on glaciers begins in November, and that determines the program up to January.

Depending on snow cover, the first short practice tours can start in December or January with the chosen climbing aids. Because of thin snow cover the snowboard should be left at home. In addition to more frequent tours with climbing aids riders can take numerous runs on the snowboard under various trail conditions to improve coordination and technique.

The best time for freeriders is from the end of January through the middle of May, depending on how the winter goes. In this time frame tours become longer and more technically demanding. If a rider has set a major goal as a challenge, it should fall in the last third of the touring season.

GETTING READY FOR A FREERIDING TRIP

Before deciding to take a Freeriding tour, it's a good idea to evaluate objectively your abilities and individual requirements. Beginners should seek the aid of qualified guides. The planning and execution of a tour calls for unconditional consideration for safety and nature. Accumulating experiences in the alpine winter, the safety equipment, and a low acceptance of risk contribute to safety. This ground rule is still often forgotten in snowboarding. Neglect of safety considerations is dangerous to oneself and to others.

Conducting a tour on your own requires lots of experience. Even experienced freeriders are not immune to the dangers of the mountains. Qualified guides are a good idea for advanced freeriders, and practically mandatory for beginners. That ensures the necessary safety and make it possible to gain experience.

Freeriding beginners, and even experienced freeriders, should consider having a qualified mountaineering and skiing guide lead their tour.

Maps and Guidebooks

Once a rider has chosen an area, the planning begins with the acquisition of appropriate maps and guidebooks that are available in bookstores or direct from mountain climbing associations. These are good places to ask further questions. You can pick up guidebooks that explain the time frames for individual trips. After establishing the route, which always depends on consideration of nature and safety, the altitudes that must be overcome are identified in the maps. That yields the precise time frame of the trip, which should provide for ample reserve time.

Further Important Sources of Information

For midrange planning, weather information should be gathered a week before the start of the tour. Information on local snow and avalanche areas is available by phone. Before starting the tour this information must be updated. It is crucial to the choice and completion of any route.

Information on Weather

Weather Conditions

Contact local radio stations, the U.S. Weather Service, and local chambers of commerce for weather conditions. Individual ski resorts can supply information for their areas as well.

Road Conditions

State and local police and the Highway Patrol can provide information on road conditions.

For laying out climbing routes and descents, good maps and a compass are essential.

Avalanche Reports

Since 1993 avalanche danger has been ranked on a five-step scale that contains additional information on terrain conditions deemed critical to avalanches. These include altitude, exposure, and shape of terrain, among others. The term Steep Slope applies to slopes 30° or greater (see chart at right). **Beginners and less experienced riders should tour only at danger levels 1 and 2.**

Travel and Transfer

If the departure and destination points of single or multiday tours are not the same, return to the starting point must be included in the planning. For longer hikes in late spring, mountain bikes may serve transportation needs. Travel to the touring area should be gentle on the environment. Often planned destinations can be reached by rail and bus.

Use of public transportation for travel and transfer is an important contribution to protecting the environment.

Traveling by Mountain Bike

This option is particularly attractive in late spring when the snow has disappeared from the valleys. A mountain bike can shorten the time needed for climbing and return. For touring on flat roads through long valleys, a bike is a sensible means of transportation, and it's also fun. Don't forget to bring a helmet for the descent. You should also bring some light mountain biking shoes and a small tool kit with some replacement parts.

Don't overlook the increased weight of your equipment during the trip in. Ride in low gear. If your body uses up too much energy on the trip in, the rest of the trip could be jeopardized.

Danger Level		Snow Cover Stability
1	minimal	Snow cover is generally well packed and stable.
2	moderate	Snow cover is only moderately well packed on some steep slopes, otherwise generally well packed.
3	high	Snow cover is only moderately to loosely packed on many steep slopes.
4	great	Snow cover is loosely packed on most steep slopes.
5	very great	Snow cover is generally loosely packed and very unstable.

Danger Level	Avalanche Probability	Advice for Tourists
1	Avalanche is possible only with much added stress on a few, very steep slopes. Only small spontaneous slides are likely.	Mostly safe touring conditions.
2	Probable avalanche with much added stress, especially on certain steep slopes. Not much danger of larger spontaneous avalanches.	Favorable touring conditions, but pay attention to local danger areas.
3	Probable avalanche with minimal added stress, especially on steep slopes. Some spontaneous, medium-to-large avalanches possible.	Snowboarding tours require experience and judgment with avalanches. Touring possibilities are restricted.
4	An avalanche is probable on most steep slopes. May be many medium or multiple and large avalanches.	Snowboard touring requires great judgment in regard to avalanches. Touring possibilities are greatly restricted.
5	Spontaneous and numerous large avalanches even on moderately steep terrain.	Snowboard touring generally not possible.

CLIMBING

Important Considerations Before Starting

Before the climb you should become thoroughly familiar with routes, possible difficulties, climbing time, and rest points. Check over the equipment again. Verify that the avalanche beacons are working properly. Food should be easily accessible. Climbing speed is regulated to the least fit participant in the group. Hiking speed should be slow enough to permit easy breathing through the nose. Warm-up time is about twenty to thirty minutes. Thereafter the muscles and circulatory system are ready for a higher cadence.

The safety of the group takes precedence over all trail considerations. Following the leader's track is especially important in critical snow conditions. Adequate rest stops must be built into long climbs.

Hiking Technique

Walking with Skis or Snowshoes

Climbing with snowshoes or skis is easier because of the greater surface area of both systems and because of the forward gliding afforded by skis. Snowshoes and climbing skins on skis make climbing more like normal walking.

Climbing skins prevent sliding backward while climbing on skis. It's important to fit them precisely to the skis. Climbing skins become less effective on ice and hard-pack. Crampons can take over some of the work in such conditions. With snowshoes backsliding is prevented by the mesh and the ice points.

A good and rhythmic walking technique is achieved by weighting the one ski heavily while the other one is pushed forward on the snow by the opposite leg without lifting. Because there is no glide with snowshoes, the advancing leg must be actively lifted. Length of stride with both systems should be set to create a rhythmic weight change, dependent upon steepness of the slope. The climbing track should be set at hip width whether skis or snowshoes are used.

If skis are canted in climbing on hard-pack, reduced contact by the climbing skins results in backsliding. Therefore skis should be set down flat.

In contrast to hiking with skis, snowshoes should choose a track closer to the fall line, since the snowshoes can hardly be placed flat on a diagonal line in steep terrain. On long, steep passages this technique requires lots of conditioning and experience with snowshoes.

Climbing aids are useful on skis in steep terrain. They keep the bindings from sinking in too much.

Travel speed should be regulated according to physical capabilities, the terrain, and the snow cover. This should always be accounted for in the planning. Physical stress can be greatly accentuated while cutting a trail. On a tough trail the order of climbers should be changed from time to time.

To achieve a more moderate pitch to the trail, build in some turns, or in steeper terrain, some switchbacks.

In a turn, tips and tails of skis or snowshoes are turned out of the track and into the hill and set down. To maintain a moderate rhythm, wide turns are preferable to switchbacks. In quick climbs in steep terrain it's easier to set the turns with the support of telescoping ski poles. Switchbacks require a good sense of balance and must be mastered by freeriders. The track should be made flat just before and during the turns.

There is a difference between uphill and downhill turns. In moderately steep terrain the uphill turn is used. In extremely steep terrain the downhill turn is used to avoid the danger of falling backward. With snowshoes the downhill turn doesn't apply, since in steep terrain it's usual to follow the fall line quite closely. In steep terrain the uphill telescoping ski pole can be held under the grip.

Climbing on Foot

Climbing mountain peaks must often be done on foot or with crampons because of the steepness. On medium-hard snow, soft boot freeriders using crampons are often forced to turn back because of the soft material of their boots. This must be foreseen in the tour plan; otherwise there is increased danger of taking a fall.

The climb follows the fall line. The climber lightly kicks notches in the snow with the boot to form steps whose surface supports at least half the length of the boot. Once this depth can no longer be achieved, crampons are needed even with hard boots. The body's center of gravity shifts from foot to foot. This is easier with a body position that's as upright as possible.

Climbers should not lean into the slope; otherwise their foot will slide out of the step. With harder snow the steps are cut by kicking harder with the lower leg.

Walking with Crampons

Only the essential points of crampon technique will be presented in the following paragraphs.

A complete introduction to all techniques can be found in other sources. Dedicated freeriders who would like to venture into glacial regions should have at their disposal a basic understanding of crampon technique.

For freeriders the vertical point technique in combination with crossover steps is normally adequate. With this technique all vertical points of the crampons are put into contact with the ground and weighted. With legs at hip-width, the feet angle out slightly and are placed so that all crampon points contact the surface simultaneously. Length of stride is set so that balance is always maintained. Steps become shorter as the terrain gets steeper.

In descending with crampons you make a pronounced weight shift onto the weight-bearing leg.

A great danger consists of catching a tooth of a crampon on the pants or straps of another crampon while walking, since that can lead to a stumble or a fall. Therefore the following points must be observed:

- Keep feet hip-width apart while climbing
- Keep feet hip-width apart while descending and angle the feet outward for stability

It may also be helpful to use gaiters on the lower legs, since they help contain baggy wind pants and keep them out of harm's way as crampons pass with each stride. Freeriders who anticipate using crampons should consult published resources or experienced back country travelers. A guided tour under the direction of a professional would be a good way to learn crampon technique. If you must rely on your own resources to learn, it's always a good idea to practice before undertaking a freeriding trip when the progress and enjoyment of others will depend on your proficiency.

An energy-efficient climbing technique is essential for the subsequent descent.

PATHFINDING

Slab avalanches pose the greatest danger to snowboarders.

Preliminary Observations on Avalanches

The nature of snow holds many uncertainties that accompany freeriders on every tour. The acceptance of these uncertainties and deliberate analysis are the basic requirement for setting trails for climbing and descending. The following observations are only a glimpse into this very complex theme. They're the first step toward a safe start in this endeavor and should motivate riders to further their understanding.

Snow is not merely snow. Behind this rather trite-sounding statement lurks the greatest danger for freeriders. That leads us to the differences among avalanches. It's important to know the basic difference between loose snow avalanches and slab avalanches in order to evaluate the avalanche situation.

Snow changes condition as early as a couple of hours after it falls. This can be demonstrated by a simple shovel test: with loose snow conditions, the snow falls off an avalanche shovel the same way loose

gravel would. Snow texture under these conditions results in fairly harmless loose snow slides.

But if the snow has already metamorphosed, it sticks together on the shovel and falls from the blade as a lump. This change makes for the greatest dangers for freeriders. The great majority of freerider avalanches are "soft slabs" of very soft to soft layers of compressed snow. They can be triggered by misjudgments on the part of freeriders. They are like set traps with a very light trigger.

When this metamorphosis in snow conditions begins, a slope becomes like a mine field. The life-threatening dangers are comparable.

A slope can be divided into zones of high and low stability; if disturbed, the latter can cause the whole slope to break off. These "islands of instability" can't hold their own weight and play a decisive role in triggering a slab avalanche. As soon as they are disturbed, a slab falls off.

For further clarification, a slope can be envisioned as broken down into big blocks, as Munter suggests. With a homogeneous slope (mine-free), each block would carry its own weight. The entire slope would thus be stable. With a heterogeneous slope comprised of blocks that can't support their own weight (mines), the stable blocks must hold back the unstable ones against pulling, pressure, and shearing forces. The resulting tensions make for an unstable slope. The more unstable zones a slope has, the greater the probability it will break off, and the greater the danger to freeriders.

Unstable zones generally require critical mass to break up. A slope can also contain several noncritical zones and still be stable; only by traveling repeatedly over these weak points can they become connected into a critical zone. Then the slope breaks apart under some freerider.

These observations give rise to the great difficulty of evaluating existing conditions. On-the-spot analysis of snow conditions is based on sample surveys (e.g., a block slide test). But these are insufficient with unstable slopes because of the random distribution of critical zones. Generalizations on the snow situation of the entire slope are inadmissible.

Computerized Search in Snow

The triggering of avalanches, as already mentioned, is subject to the accident principle. Munter has developed a method that makes it less likely to set off avalanches. It is currently being refined and developed further. Its steps produce the freerider's increasing degree of experience. With these methods, areas containing avalanche danger are singled out by means of three so-called filters. Step by step the detail increases up to the fundamental question: To go or not to go?

Assessment of Danger is Determined by:
1. A regional filter: planning the tour at home
2. A local filter: choice of route and cutting trail while traveling in the terrain
3. A zonal filter: assessment of snow cover on individual slopes. "To go or not to go?" Yes/No determination

It's important to follow the three steps in this order. They build on one another and are interdependent.

Minimizing risk is accomplished through Munter's so-called Reduction Method. Risk potential from the avalanche report is reduced by preventive behavior that involves avoiding certain exposures and gradients. If the resulting factor for remaining risk is equal to or less than one, then the planned tour can go ahead.

The numerical value makes it possible to assess statistical risk and provides a means to make a clear decision. Risk potential increases exponentially with calculation of the danger levels of the avalanche report (see p.141).

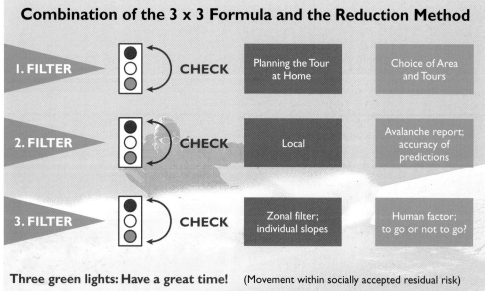

Combination of the 3 x 3 Formula and the Reduction Method

1. FILTER	CHECK	Planning the Tour at Home	Choice of Area and Tours
2. FILTER	CHECK	Local	Avalanche report; accuracy of predictions
3. FILTER	CHECK	Zonal filter; individual slopes	Human factor; to go or not to go?

Three green lights: Have a great time! (Movement within socially accepted residual risk)

Fig. 20: Schematic representation of Munter's decision-making sequence, which is similiar to a traffic light.

Regional Filter

Preparation for the climb and descent is done at home. The following elements that contribute to avalanches are decisive factors:
- Weather
- Snow cover
- Terrain

You can gather information at home about these main factors that contribute to avalanches. The weather report provides information on recent and future weather. It contains predictions on
- Intensity of precipitation
- Temperature ranges
- Wind conditions

The avalanche report provides information on the basic firmness of the snow cover. That makes it possible to conclude if you may have to deal with
- Loose snow avalanches
- Breakup of the entire snow cover

Generally the main cause of slab avalanche danger is new snow with wind. The first nice day after a period of precipitation is particularly dangerous. The criteria for evaluation are
- Amount or intensity of new snow
- Wind strength
- Temperature

The following new snow amounts create a critical situation for freeriders (at least a considerable danger of slab snow)
- 4–8 inches (10–20 centimeters) in unfavorable conditions
- 8–12 inches (20–30 centimeters) in moderate conditions
- 12–16 inches (30–40 centimeters) in good conditions

The following conditions are unfavorable
- Strong wind (over 30 mph/50 kilometers per hour)
- Low temperatures (under 18°F or -8°C), especially when cold air is moving in
- After warm periods (cold to warm)
- Glazed snow, older, or very cold layers as surface of old snow

Favorable conditions include
- Calm wind
- Temperatures not much below freezing especially at the start of snowfall, or rather a shift from rain to snow (warm on cold)

Chutes are potential avalanche routes.

Maps provide information on terrain (relief and topography), slope exposure, and steepness of slopes. The following apply to terrain
- Chutes, valleys, and ravines are potential avalanche routes.
- V-shaped valleys with north-south orientation are hazardous in the spring because of their long exposure to the sun's rays and to the consequent soaking of the snow.
- Slopes that end in a valley at their bottom must be evaluated with great care, since in such places it doesn't take much snow to bury someone.
- Ridges and terraced terrain are desirable.
- Slopes that end in level terrain are preferable to those that end abruptly, since the latter involve added risk of falling.
- Broken terrain reduces danger of avalanches.

The following dangers exist relative to exposure of the slope
- Slopes in the lee of prevailing winds are especially prone to avalanches due to shifting of snow by wind.

In areas near ridges, always proceed with caution in the lee.

The following are important considerations with respect to pitch of slope
Avalanches almost never occur on slopes of less than ten degrees.
Between 10 and 28°, avalanches are rare.
30° marks the start of danger zones for slab avalanches.
The danger zone for loose snow avalanches begins at 35°.
On slopes exceeding 45°, avalanche danger is even higher, even though there is less snow.

Freerider Factors:
With this factor freeriders are dealing with their own abilities and the way they plan. The group dynamics of a party of freeriders is very important. A competitive spirit may arise all too quickly in the group. Exposure to heightened risk is the consequence. This fact applies to experienced freeriders, too. Good riding technique is never a justification for taking excessive risk. Foresight and possible abandonment of the tour—not one's physical abilities—are the ways to deal with danger. This is what constitutes the danger for good freeriders. The better their riding technique, the greater their enthusiasm; but acceptance of danger also increases as a function of this euphoria. Knowledge of one's own behavior and how to assess it are fundamentals needed in adapting to situations that arise on every tour.

Local Filter

The second filter involves evaluation of the overall situation on the spot. This can happen only after Filter I has produced a green light for this second step. Here again there's no mistaking the fact that tour choice is determined by weather and avalanche conditions, not by the freeriders' desires.

At this point the evaluation consists of the mere examination of visible symptoms of the overall situation. Observation starts upon arrival in the area and continues throughout the entire tour. Generally the selection of climbing and descent routes is subject to the following:
Consideration of snow and weather conditions
Safety with respect to avalanches and falls (including crevasses on glaciers)
Energy-saving routes; choice of most favorable snow conditions for ascent and descent
Consideration for nature and the environment

The first two points are of particular interest here. On the subject of weather and snow conditions, the explanations given earlier should be borne in mind. The following important factors must be judged:
- Land shapes, relief, topography
- Steepness of slopes
- Exposure of slopes
- Weather

Other danger criteria are added to this list on the spot.

Freeriders have to be conscious of the greater danger involved in jumping off cornices.

Visibility:

Poor visibility is produced by fog, falling snow, diffused light, or dusk. It interferes with choosing the best route and with evaluating steepness of slopes.

Surface Qualities:

The nature of the slope's surface is another important criterion with avalanches. These are the important criteria:

- Grassy slopes and leafy forest floors make an ideal base for sliding snow
- Small shrubs and snow-covered dwarf evergreens favor buildup of loose snow
- Sparse stands of trees are an unreliable protection against avalanches
- Rough underlayers such as piles of rubble and boulders deter sliding
- Woods with sufficient undergrowth are generally good avalanche protection

Temperature and Radiation:

Temperature and radiation should be evaluated along with other local factors. Accidents often happen in the following conditions:

- Cold snowfall after a lengthy period of sunshine (clear and cold)
- Rise above freezing for the first time in several days above 3,300 feet (3000 meters)
- Warm winds that create avalanche danger on all types of slopes; this condition may be short-lived because of the rapid unloading of the slopes. (With an overcast sky warming is often greater than people think.)

- Cooling off from afternoon to evening after intense sunshine and warming that cause only an apparent and deceptive stabilization

Safe avalanche conditions are likely only after rapid softening of snow followed by a very cold night.

Frequenting Slopes:

Another criterion for evaluation in this filter is the frequency and regularity of crossing a slope under conditions of critical snow amount (see p.146). Slopes that are crossed only rarely under these conditions are classified as unfavorable to further access. On the other hand, slopes that were used often and regularly prior to this situation are less dangerous.

Zonal Filter

A further refinement in avalanche reporting is reached with the zonal filter. This concerns evaluation of the snow cover's load-bearing capacity on specific slopes. This filter requires the most experience on the part of the freerider. It involves the greatest degree of difficulty in assessment. It's of great importance with valid doubts, especially with thin snow cover. Freeriders should include all their gathered knowledge (filters 1 and 2) in the zonal filter as they do the present evaluation. That's the basis for the final determination: "To go or not to go?"

This determination is supported by analysis of load-bearing capacity at safe but representative locations. The following are analyzed:

- The steepest slope (see p.147)
- Cohesion, e.g., snow that sticks together on critical sliding surfaces (see shovel test, p.144)
- Firmness of base as determined by snow profile and block slide test

Following intense sunshine, afternoon cooling often leads to apparent stabilization of the slope.

For closer evaluation of base firmness the so-called snow cover tests (block slide test and snow profile) are very important. They won't be explained further here, since their use should be learned from an expert. They contribute to safety only with constant use. Freeriders who venture forth without the services of official guides should master these tests. If it appears that a snow cover test is called for, it should be done without hesitation.

Every change among layers within the snow cover creates a new potential sliding surface. Critical layers, or gliding surfaces are

```
Contact surfaces between old and
new snow (the most common case)
Snow-covered surface frost as a
loose intermediate layer (deep
frost, usually cold on warm)
Contact surfaces between loose
snow layer and layer above it
Snow-covered glaze or ice layers
Snow-covered dust (yellow or
reddish-yellow dust)
```

This knowledge then yields the main question:
```
To what extent can one transpose
steepness, altitude, exposure,
ridge structures and frequency of
crossing to comparable slopes?
```

Especially with filters 2 and 3 the following ground rules apply to freeriders:
```
Pause and take your time.
Think through and organize the
situation.
Set priorities: What must happen?
What must not happen?
```

The three filters clarify the increasing difficulty of evaluating situations. That gets better only through continuous use and refinement. The complexity of evaluating conditions lies on the one hand in the continual interaction among individual danger factors, and on the other hand, in the evaluation of these factors in time and place, and in the resulting final determination. Over time, the goal of the freerider should be to become acquainted with as many factors as possible that cause or reduce danger. That leads to greater caution. In Freeriding, courage is often a lack of insight, whereas cowardice is often based on sound information.

Freeriders are motivated by fun, challenges, and excitement. Safety should never be overlooked, though, and the desire to ride new terrain should not

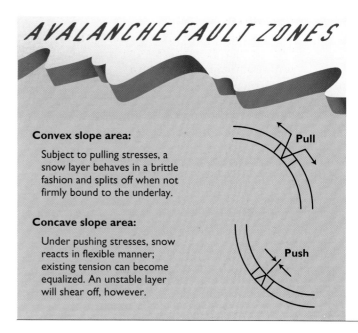

Fig. 21: Effect of slope shape on snow cover.

Convex slope area:
Subject to pulling stresses, a snow layer behaves in a brittle fashion and splits off when not firmly bound to the underlay.

Concave slope area:
Under pushing stresses, snow reacts in flexible manner; existing tension can become equalized. An unstable layer will shear off, however.

be stronger than the voice of common sense. One should never underestimate the power of nature; and in the face of treacherous avalanche conditions, rapidly changing weather, poor visibility, excessive fatigue, exposed ledge, or otherwise inauspicious terrain, riders must not persist despite their best judgment.

Walking and Riding on Glaciers

A special form of touring with the snowboard is walking and riding on glaciers. Walking onto a glacier always requires bringing along glacier equipment (see Special Equipment for the Freerider). A glacier tour does not always involve linking climbers by rope.

Glacier and terrain characteristics, as well as prevailing snow and visibility conditions, are decisive reasons for or against using ropes for ascent and descent (see p.150). In any case, using ropes and locating a person who has fallen into a crevasse should be learned from an expert.

As always, prior practice under conditions less demanding than those encountered on a freeriding expedition is advised. Knot-tying with gloved or cold hands may become the order of the day. General rope know-how and specific techniques should be mastered by all members of the party in case conditions require their use.

Glacial cracks, or glaciers with lots of fissures _____

Poor visibility _____

New snow, particularly after the wind has moved it around _____

Ropes can be dispensed with
- On deep, old snow, or frozen snow
- On glaciers known since preceding summer to be free of crevasses

Using ropes on the descent requires added riding skills of the freerider and therefore should be considered as early as the planning stages. Secure rope technique and advancing in the ropes must in any case be learned in a course or from an expert.

The trail over a glacier should, to the extent possible, go through areas devoid of crevasses. Often terrain characteristics indicate where crevasse areas are located.

High frequency of crevasses may be expected

On steep terrain at end of glacier _____

On steep, powerful, and fast-flowing glaciers _____

On outside curve areas of large glaciers ____

In powerful feeding zones of large glaciers __

In case of doubt even experienced freeriders should venture onto a glacier only with an official guide.

Avalanche Rescues

Despite the most modern devices, recovering people alive from avalanches is still a matter of luck. The chances of rescue from an avalanche depend essentially on
- How long the person has been buried
- How deep the person is buried
- Terrain
- Proper first aid

Fig. 22 illustrates the declining chances of survival of a person buried in an avalanche as a function of elapsed time. Experience shows that lack of oxygen (suffocation) is the most frequent cause of death for people buried in an avalanche.

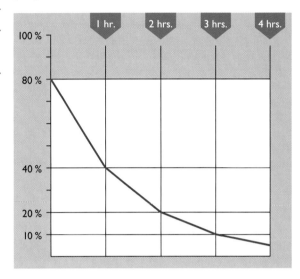

Fig. 22: Survival chances after being buried in an avalanche.

The following self-help points are effective in reducing risk of avalanche accidents:

- In an avalanche, the snowboard works like an anchor. Getting free of the board is difficult. There is danger of severe twisting and straining of ankles and joints (e.g., ruptured tendons and bone fractures).
- Only very good freeriders will be able to outrun small avalanches. Flight will never work during the ascent.
- As long as the avalanche is in motion, you can resist getting buried.
- Before the avalanche ceases moving the victim should try to assume a crouching position and create breathing space with the hands.
- If no daylight gets through to the buried person, relief efforts and calling are futile.
- Under the snow it is therefore advisable to use the available oxygen as sparingly as possible and not to lose faith in the rescue.

The other tour participants help by conducting a competent search with the locator devices (see p.128). There are systematic search pattern for individuals and groups that should be learned thoroughly.

First-Aid Measures

The greatest threat to a buried person is posed by suffocation. The head should therefore be freed first so that artificial respiration can be given, if necessary. But artificial respiration should not interfere with further digging. Victims who are rescued conscious still need to be handled with extreme care. They should not move. Hypothermia is an important factor during rescue.

Buried persons usually don't cool down too much while in the snow, but rather after being removed from it. They should therefore be wrapped up in a bivouac sack, for example, to keep them warm. They should be given no medicines, but only warm, sweetened drinks without alcohol.

Organized Rescue

Independent of the equipment and associated possibilities for immediate rescue, the following are of prime importance in avalanche accidents:

Marking the points where the person was caught, disappeared, and is suspected to lie buried

Searching with eyes and ears; carefully search accident site to see if the victim or pieces of equipment are sticking out of the snow

If these measures and the ensuing search with electronic locators don't find the victim, a large-scale rescue operation is the only recourse.

Rescue by Rescue Team

The information on rescue teams refers to the following important questions:
- What happened?
- When did it happen?
- Precisely where?
- Who, or how many people, are buried?

For rescue by helicopter, the following information is also important:
- Who is reporting from where?
- Precisely where is the accident site, and is it possible to land?
- What's the weather like in the accident area (clear or overcast, altitude of underside of cloud cover, wind direction and speed, type of snow)?

The following are important signals for helicopter pilots (see Fig. 23):

Yes

We need help.

Yes to questions dropped to the ground.

Land here.

No

We don't need help.

No to questions dropped.

Don't land.

Fig. 23: Communicating with helicopter pilot.

ON BOARD

Freeriding has lots of faces when it comes to riding technique. The continually changing conditions on a tour and the great physical demands have an effect on a freerider's technical ability. Anyone who's looking for the absolute experience should focus on these conditions.

Safety places great demands on riding technique (see Pathfinding). Riders who can't master their board under all conditions should cut back on their tour planning.

Good freeriders possess well-developed motor skills. They immediately adapt their riding technique to quickly changing conditions. During the descent freeriders get continuous sensitive feedback on the ride of their board and adjust themselves to the existing situation.

It's not possible to prescribe a riding style in Freeriding. Riding style is different for every freerider, based on physical characteristics and inner views.

The following observations concern typical conditions as the freerider often encounters them. They should be complemented by further explanations from racing and Freestyle, and inspire riders to accumulate more experience in the realm of technique while still observing safe practices. Individuality is of paramount importance in Freeriding technique, but these liberties must always be consistent with safety and nature.

Position on the Board

Even in Freeriding the body's center of gravity is generally over both legs, which are weighted evenly. In wet and difficult snow conditions or in many situations in deep snow, where the board tip threatens to dig in, the center of gravity should be shifted carefully to the hind leg.

At high cadence the center of gravity can be lowered by bending the knees more to smooth out uneven spots. This applies especially to riding while carrying fairly heavy equipment.

Effect of Equipment Weight

According to terrain, all types of technique that must be mastered will have an application. The weight of a backpack can detract from riding technique on long (multiday) tours. The higher overall weight of the freerider has a direct impact on how the board handles. Under the circumstances the tension and stiffness of the board based on body weight are inadequate, so the board breaks loose on hard and icy surfaces. In such cases a stiffer board is recommended.

Powder

For riding in deep snow, the feeling for the movement is crucial. The deeper and softer the snow, the more sensitive and measured the freerider's technique should be (as in straightening the legs). That's how to experience "powder flash" properly.

At higher speeds the board picks up more flotation until it glides on the soft surface of the snow. Then it possesses its ability to turn, and even at high tempo it's possible to change directions as needed. If the nose of the board takes a dive (the board "grabs"), the center of gravity should be carefully shifted to the rear leg. Strong balancing motions should be avoided in deep snow because of the heightened danger of falling. Swing turns are characterized by a harmonious and rhythmic motion.

Riding in Firn

The most important point to keep in mind about riding on firn is the variable and often very high resistance to turning due to the nature of the snow. It requires great flexibility to compensate for the turn resistance. This is accomplished primarily by dynamic leg work. In heavy, wet snow the center of gravity should be carefully shifted to the hind leg. Edge pressure in turning should likewise be applied carefully.

Riding in Crusty Snow

Freeriders encounter the quickest-changing conditions in crusty snow. Breaking through the crust often disturbs the freerider's balance and rhythm. Sometimes that leads to unpleasant falls.

Riding in crusty snow therefore requires a very dynamic, consistent, and flexible style. The demands on the leg muscles are particularly high under these conditions. Muscular fatigue is surely a reason to stop for a rest.

Riding in crusty snow presents the quickest-changing conditions.

Riding Steep Slopes

Riding steep slopes involves the most difficult conditions for Freeriding technique. That's why it should be done only by the most experienced freeriders. Often these slopes exceed 45° in ravines or gullies. The slopes are usually avalanche-free because of their steepness and have a hard, icy base. Another difficulty is the narrowness of many steep ravines.

Under extremely icy conditions or with a heavy backpack, the steepest part should be negotiated by side-slipping. If the surface can be ridden, exaggerated jump turns should be used. Here it's important to get a good leap from the strongly bent legs and end the movement with a new deep knee bend. This is possible only with very high edge pressure. The board is immediately placed diagonally across the fall line like in a one-eighty. The body's center of gravity should be as nearly as possible over the slope-side edge to avoid the threat of a fall. As the slope becomes wider and less steep, the swing radii can be increased and the jump phases of the turns can be reduced.

Riding in Rocky Terrain

In rocky terrain, which can exist due to lack of snow, or even with plenty of snow with big boulders, it's important to anticipate where the trail will lead. Especially at higher tempo the rider should follow a line that corresponds to conditions. Riders who exceed circumstances may risk a lift-threatening fall on a boulder. During the climb the freerider should commit to memory the approximate riding line in

"Powder flash": the feeling is supreme.

While riding in rocky terrain, jumps over small boulders can be done only with very good snow cover and riding technique.

technique and therefore the freerider's safety. In areas where a fall could be dangerous, the freerider's riding technique and concentration are challenged to the utmost. Board control takes absolute precedence over speed. This is especially true of riding in poor visibility.

As already explained, freeriders should possess excellent riding technique if they are to ride while using the ropes (see Walking and Riding on Glaciers). Because of the relatively high instability on the board (riding on one edge), it doesn't take much of a pull on the rope to destroy a rider's stable riding position. Often that leads to a fall. Riding on a track, for instance, in critical snow conditions or on glaciers, requires a great degree of concentration and balance. In all these areas, controlled riding speed is the most important thing. Frequent pauses are needed in cases of extreme fatigue.

Hits

In general, hits can be done only with great care in Freeriding. Added risk of injury is to be avoided at all costs. Previous examination of takeoff and landing areas is essential and is based on the mentioned safety criteria. With adequate safety (no avalanche danger) hits in steep terrain are preferable to ones on flat slopes because of the risk of injury posed by the hard landing in the latter case (see p.109ff.).

Concerning avalanche danger, we should mention the inviting cornices that frequently occur in back country. Freeriders who jump over these insidious traps without checking them out risk their own lives and maybe those of others.

So hits off cornices are suited only to extremely experienced freeriders who have a firm grasp of the danger situation. The slightest doubt in the freerider's mind also means that caution takes highest priority.

The additional weight of the equipment can have a major effect on technique in hits. In any case, straight hits are preferable to spin tricks. In the best, absolutely safe conditions, and with sufficient reserve time for the tour, the backpack can be taken off (but never the avalanche beacon) for repeated hits at the same spot. Even under the safest conditions the other freeriders should remain prepared for emergencies.

Freeriders who experience fear in anticipation of a jump should pass it up. The danger of injury is too great. Jumps over boulders or cliffs are permissible only with absolutely secure and adequate snow cover. Riders who misjudge this may risk their lives.

conjunction with climbing and descent routes. Taking a descent route different from the climbing route necessitates repeated stops to check out the terrain. Jumps over small boulders are feasible only with very good snow cover; otherwise there is great danger of injury on the rocky ground.

Difficult Conditions

Aside from the conditions already mentioned that freeriders encounter on a tour, there are other factors that can detract from their riding skills. Here too the aspect of safety is of greatest importance. These additional complications can crop up singly or in combinations. The more of them there are, the greater the stress on the freerider. This fact must be considered in planning the tour (see p.140).

The following conditions can interfere with riding technique:

- Riding in flat terrain (fatigue factor)
- Riding while very tired
- Riding in terrain where there is greater danger of falling
- Riding in poor visibility
- Riding while using ropes
- Riding in the track

Riding in flat terrain can be linked to greater physical effort. It thus presents an indirect danger factor in the form of fatigue. Great fatigue detracts from riding

NATURE CONSERVANCY

The Unconditional Price for the Freeriding Experience

Under absolutely safe conditions the backpack—but never the avalanche beacon—can be set aside for several hits at the same spot.

Disregard for nature means sooner or later the end of Freeriding, and perhaps of all snowboarding. Conservation is an essential planning factor in Freeriding trips.

A snowboarding tour becomes an unforgettable nature experience when the participants are concerned with nature. Comprehensive knowledge of the ecological consequences of inappropriate behavior is therefore essential to showboarders. It allows them to carry out their responsibility to nature.

Travel

Many touring areas offer the possibility of using public transportation. Prior planning makes it possible to travel without harming the environment. The endangered alpine environment is spared from harmful gases if an automobile is not used. If use of private automobiles can't be avoided, at least car pools should be set up.

Damage to Vegetation

Young trees are particularly susceptible to damage from Freeriding. Totally or partially covered with snow, they are easily overlooked during the climb and descent. Snowboard edges can damage side shoots, tops, and stems; sometimes small trees can be cut right off. If nature cannot regenerate, the forest's second growth and accompanying avalanche protection are threatened. For that reason, stands of young trees are absolutely off-limits to freeriders.

Freeriding can cause damage to young trees.

Trash

Trash endangers the sensitive wilderness in many ways. Under no circumstances should freeriders leave trash in the wilderness. Conservation and touring can be combined only when criteria for environmental friendliness are considered in planning and execution. We live in partnership with nature and not apart from it. Freeriders are always encouraged to become thoroughly familiar with nature and environmental conservancy.

Damage is also done to root systems of older trees and in scrub and dwarf tree stands (mountain pines and rhododendrons). Damage from edges and foot traffic poses increased danger to turf on alpine meadows when snow cover is thin. Therefore freeriders should refrain from touring if the snow is not deep enough, or at least take off the board and walk through problem areas.

Here are the main points:

- Minimize stress produced by driving automobiles.
- Observe markers, notices, and zoning concepts.
- Avoid damaging vegetation.
- Go easy on wild animals.
- Keep the wilderness clean.

Wild Animals and Birds

Freeriders are a disturbance in the habitat of wild animals, especially deer. There is a difference in the intensity of the disturbance during climbing and descending. Animals act fairly composed to freeriders who are climbing. But if an animal is surprised by a descending snowboarder, it is startled and panics. The result is strength-sapping flight with increased energy expenditure. If tracks lead you to suspect presence of wild animals, better not ride those slopes. Cut a wide berth around grazing areas. Given safe avalanche conditions, north- and north-westerly-facing slopes are preferable, as long as they are not home territory to wildlife. Some types of endangered birds whose biotope is very specific don't feed adequately when disturbed. This includes black grouse, hazel grouse, and others. You can learn to recognize their habitat. These areas should be avoided whenever possible.

Endangered birds are sensitive to disturbance from freeriders.

Disturbances lead to strength-sapping flight and to increased energy expenditure.

Board
tuning

Whether in high-speed racing, Freestyle big airs, or Freeriding in powder—riding safety, the sensation of movement, and the experience of riding are achieved only through appropriate board tuning. That's vitally important **in the entire sport of snowboarding!**

Equipment care is an important part of general training (see p.30).

It's crucial to all aspects of snowboarding, not just in competition. Its importance is noticeable as a motivational component in technique training, conditioning, enjoyment of riding, and success. Well-prepared equipment also contributes significantly to riding safety.

Gliding and Factors that Affect It

Information on weather and snow conditions before training or competition are the most important factors for board preparation. Because of their complexity, they are deciding factors in many situations. The problem lies in conditions that vary widely. The following are determining factors:

- Temperature
- Humidity
- Snow granulation
- Wind
- Radiational warming

Movement of the snowboard, that is, gliding of the board on the snow, is based on the physical properties of friction and warming. Snow particles melt with gliding. Between the waxed base and the top of the snow water droplets are produced that act like grease.

The quality of this effect can be influenced significantly by the choice of wax and by the structure of the base. The running surface is adapted to the respective snow conditions by means of the wax; at the same time, it is subject to abrasion. Unwaxed bases make for fairly high abrasion; that produces a thicker film of water under the board and a suction effect that dampens speed.

The adaptation of wax to existing conditions controls abrasion and the extent of the water layer. The snow should be just a little harder than the wax. For most wax systems, there are detailed charts that make it possible to get just the right mix for prevailing conditions. Information on the influencing factors previously mentioned should still be obtained. Since snow is very abrasive at low temperature and humidity, waxes for cold temperatures are harder.

Base

The base is polished at the factory by machines. That imparts a pattern to the surface that counteracts surface tension in the film of water created by friction. The base structure also reduces contact with the snow surface and abrasion. A base glides poorly when it

- Appears very smooth, shiny, and "burned"
- Gets sealed up through heat or high pressure from the polisher
- Is oxidized and dried out for lack of wax

On most bases there is a linear or a mixed linear structure. With dry snow and low temperatures, or with cold and fresh new snow, a fine structure is needed. Medium structures are suited to somewhat older snow and rounded crystals. These are the most common snow types and temperatures. With wet snow conditions at the freezing point and higher, thicker water films are created; their suction can be broken by a rough pattern.

Plastics oxidize with UV rays, oxygen, and environmental influences. Also an unused board is subject to this change process. Waxing the board protects it. Polyethylene surfaces must be completely flat. A base that has been polished unevenly makes the board unstable and increases the danger of cutting in. The result is a major effect on the way it handles.

Flat-polishing the running surface is done mechanically with stone polishers or belt sanders. These polishers cover most snow conditions. It's often necessary to touch up the texture manually and to adapt it to prevailing conditions. The following are used for that purpose:

- special silicon carbide sandpaper (100–80 grit) with a backing block
- Wire brushes (e.g., steel, copper, and bronze)
- Texture rulers
- Nylon brushes

Fig. 24: With concave running surfaces (a) the board turns poorly and cuts in easily. Abrasion of wax on the edges is excessive. Convex running surfaces (b) cause poor handling of the board and make it unstable.

The surface is best prepared for waxing by opening its microstructural amorphous parts by means of heat from a waxing iron. That way the wax can penetrate the surface better.

Proper care of the board's surface results in better performance on the snow and longer surface life. Visual inspection of the surface will tell you when you have a gouge that needs filling or when you need to clean and wax. A few simple tools and some commercially available cleaners and waxes used regularly will keep your board performing like new. The following information will add to your enjoyment and help you get the most out of your equipment.

Cleaning the Running Surface

There are several possibilities for cleaning the running surface:

- Heat cleaning
- Liquid wax remover
- Steel scraper or draw knife

Heat Cleaning

With this method, soft, penetrating waxes are ironed into the board surface until it is warmed up. After that, the wax is removed from the surface while still warm. This process is repeated two to three times. The last time, the wax is left on the surface for fifteen to twenty minutes, and then is scraped off with a Plexiglas blade under light pressure. At the start, the texture of the surface should be freshened up with a bronze or copper brush.

Liquid Wax Removers

Especially with liquid wax removers, there are some important safety precautions on the packaging. Before applying the cleaning solution, remove old wax by scraping with a Plexiglas blade. The wax remover is applied and allowed to work in. The surface is then rubbed with a dust-free paper towel. This process is repeated as often as necessary. Before applying new wax, the surface should be allowed to dry thoroughly (about twenty minutes).

Scraping the Running Surface

After riding on extremely cold and aggressive new snow or on artificial snow, the surface is often dry, white, and seemingly "burned." What you're looking at is polyethylene fibers that have been ripped from the surface by ice crystals. This "burned" running surface should be scraped with a sharp steel scraper. After refreshing the texture with a machine or manually, the scraped-off polyethylene whiskers must be removed. They are removed with a sharp draw knife without disturbing the pattern.

Surface Repair

Riding produces small scratches and scars on the running surface. You can remove smaller holes in the surface yourself. After the board has been smoothed off with a scraper or draw knife, the surface is gone over with a bronze or copper brush.

For repairs to small gouges, flammable repair sticks are used; for greater damage, flameless meltable plastic sticks are used. In that case, the fluid material is dripped onto the damages area. With inflammable repair sticks the flame should cease smoking before the melted material is applied. After that, the surface is brushed once again (from tip to tail) and perhaps touched up with sandpaper (320-grit).

Edge Tuning

A snowboard's edges are subjected to extreme pressure in riding. Different uses require different types of edges.

As already mentioned, the running surface should be flat. This is also true for the joint between edge and running surface. With many new boards, it happens that the edge or the surface sticks up (see Fig. 25). The projecting areas should always be polished mechanically in the interests of the board's turning qualities.

For fine-tuning of edges, there are precise edge sharpening devices, special files, and polishing stones for uneven spots. You should practice with these a lot. Pay particular attention to

- Removal of uneven spots with the polishing stone before actually sharpening the edges
- Using the sharpening devices in direction of nose to tail

In Freestyle, edges are used with the existing 90° angle or with an angle of 88–89°. In this case the edge is polished off 1 to 2° on the running-surface side (see Fig. 26).

In racing the edges are ground back up to 6° on the sides for a good grip on ice. In addition, the edges can be ground as much as 4° on the running-surface side.

Tuning also depends on the technique of the individual rider. After sharpening the edges they are deburred with a Gummi Stone.

Breaking the edges into forward and rear sections involves about 8 inches (20 centimeters) for Freestyle boards and between 2 and 4 inches (5–10 centimeters) for race boards. For racing, it's advisable to polish the running surface with a fine polishing stone. That gets rid of burrs and scratches in the surface of the edges and enhances the turning qualities of the board. Edge rusting can be prevented by applying an edge-protecting film after sharpening or riding. For that purpose the edges should be dry.

Riding the board on the slopes is not the only source of enjoyment and satisfaction this sport offers. Serious riders must learn to appreciate the totality of the experience, including proper care and tuning of the edges. The dividends lie in enhanced performance and even in potential resale value.

Waxing the Board

Waxing the board properly is not just a decisive factor in competition; it also contributes to overall motivation and fun.

The choice of wax and waxing technique depends on the rider's level and objectives.

Types of Wax

The type of wax involves the factors that influence gliding mentioned earlier. Another important point is the cost factor and the energy investment.

The two types of waxes are:
- Hot waxes
- Cold waxes (powder, paste, liquid)

Hot Waxes

Hot waxes are best applied with a special iron that ensures a constant wax temperature. Waxing irons distribute the wax evenly on the running surface and ensure the best possible penetration and saturation of the surface by the wax. Hot waxes include numerous waxing systems. They differ according to manufacturer.

So-called universal waxes are suited to average conditions and designed for a broad temperature range. These economical waxes are good for basic board care or use in training. Price level and performance of the remaining hot waxes are determined principally by fluorocarbon content. Pure fluorocarbons or highly fluorided waxes are extremely water- and dirt-resistant and they enhance gliding, especially in difficult snow conditions such as wet, dirty, or new snow. In extremely low temperatures the advantage of high fluorocarbon

Fig. 26:
(a) Grinding 1–2° from the bottom of the edge make the board easier to turn.

(b) Edges ground back to as much as 84° grab well on ice.

(c) A complete tuning provides best edge performance.

Fig. 25: Possible connections between running surface and edges on new boards. The transition should be flat, as in (a). The two other forms should be modified to conform to this one.

content diminishes. But in high humidity it markedly improves gliding even at low temperatures. For extremely aggressive snow (artificial snow and very cold new snow), waxes are further provided with hard synthetic paraffins. Special forms of wax are pure fluorocarbon wax and graphite wax. The former are conceived especially for racing, and in powder form they are indispensable for rubbing onto the running surface before a race. They are very fast and work well in a broad range of temperatures.

Graphite waxes are appropriate when humidity is under 50 percent. They protect the wax from abrasion by snow crystals and increase glide. But for best effect the chosen waxes should not contain too much graphite. The proportion of graphite can be reduced by combining with graphite-free waxes. The various wax types are usually divided into different temperature categories, or are mixed to match different temperatures. The choice of these waxes is keyed to the factors just mentioned and to the manufacturers' waxing charts.

Cold Waxes

Cold waxes complement the hot waxes. They are usually available in liquid or solid form. Cold waxes are like a universal wax because of their wide temperature range. They are also easy to apply between runs in a race. These waxes should be applied once or twice a day. After application they are smoothed out. Because they're easy to carry, cold waxes are suited to long Freeriding trips. With the addition of a polishing cloth they add a lot to the fun of riding.

Applying Hot Wax

This process presumes that the previous explained steps of cleaning, repairing, texturing, and edge tuning have been done.

Maximum wax absorption of the running surface is accomplished at a temperature no higher than about 250°F (120°C). This means a maximum waxing iron temperature of about 300°F (150°C), since the temperature goes down a little in the ironing process. Only the hard synthetic paraffin waxes require such high temperatures. With softer waxes the temperature can be reduced a little. Before ironing out, there should be a good amount of wax on the surface to prevent burns. The stick of wax is either held against the bottom of the waxing iron to let it drip onto the board surface, or else heated on the iron and then rubbed onto the surface.

Here are the steps used in board preparation:

- The present racing or training wax is put on.
- Hard and brittle waxes for cold temperatures can be stripped off as long as they're slightly soft. That prevents chipping the wax layer off while it's hard.
- Extra wax is removed from the edges.
- After cooling off the running surface is scraped with a sharp Plexiglas blade under light pressure from nose to tail.
- Sides are cleaned of left-over wax and polished.
- Brush the running surface from nose to tail, e.g., with a nylon brush.
- Scrape the surface once more with the Plexiglas blade.
- Brush again with the nylon brush. With hard waxes and surfaces with fine structure, use a bronze brush too. After that, finish with the nylon brush.
- With additional application of a pure fluorocarbon powder, rub the powder in with a polisher.
- Next, brush the wax with a natural bristle brush or a soft nylon brush.
- At the start the board surface is cooled by laying the board bottom-down in the snow. Once the surface has had enough time to cool down to snow temperature, it is brushed again with a soft nylon or natural bristle brush.
- In dry powder snow the board should cool for about a half-hour. The uppermost surface contracts and part of the wax enters the surface. Before brushing, the board is once again carefully scraped with the Plexiglas blade from nose to tail.
- After use, rub the surface dry in the waxing room.
- Check over the running surface and the edges for possible damage and repair if necessary.
- Brush the surface and clean and polish if needed.
- Apply a soft wax for transport and protect the board.

Even in Freestyle competitions the last board tuning is done just before the start.

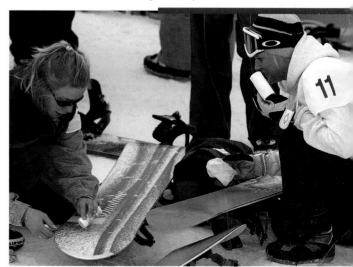

Resources

ANDERSON, B.: Stretching. Weltbild Verlag, Augsburg 1994

BAUMANN, W.: Grundlagen der Biomechanik. Studienbrief 14 der Trainerakademie Köln des Deutschen Sportbundes. Verlag Karl Hofmann, Schorndorf 1989

BOLLETTIERI, N., C. A. MAHER: Matchball. Das mentale Erfolgsprogramm von NICK BOLLETTIERI. BLV Verlagsgesellschaft, München/Wien/Zürich 1995

DAUGS, R.: Beiträge zum visuomotorischen Lernen im Sport. Verlag Karl Hofmann, Schorndorf 1989

DAUGS, R., H. MECHLING, K. BLISCHKE, H. OLIVIER: Sensomotorisches Lernen und Techniktraining. Verlag Karl Hofmann, Schorndorf 1989

DEIß, D., U. PFEIFFER: Leistungsreserven im Schnellkrafttraining. Trainingsstrategien mit Beispiellösungen in der Leichtathletik, im Skisprung und im Gewichtheben. Sportverlag, Berlin 1991

DEUTSCHER ALPENVEREIN: Protokoll der Schulung »Neue Lawinenkunde« (W. MUNTER), München 1996

EBERSPÄCHER, H.: Sportpsychologie. Grundlagen, Methoden, Analysen. Rowohlt Verlag, Reinbek 1990

EBERSPÄCHER, H.: Mentale Trainingsformen in der Praxis. Sportinform Verlag, München 1990

EHLENZ, H., M. GROSSER, E. ZIMMERMANN: Krafttraining. BLV Sportwissen. BLV Verlagsgesellschaft, München/Wien/Zürich 1995 (5)

GEYER, P., W. POHL: Eisgehen – Klettern in Eis und kombiniertem Gelände. Alpin-Lehrplan Band 3. BLV Verlagsgesellschaft, München/Wien/Zürich 1997 (3)

GEYER, P., W. POHL: Skibergsteigen – Variantenfahren. Alpin-Lehrplan Band 4. BLV Verlagsgesellschaft, München/Wien/Zürich 1997 (3)

GROSSER, M.: Schnelligkeitstraining. BLV Sportwissen. BLV Verlagsgesellschaft, München/Wien/Zürich 1991

GROSSER, M., H. MÜLLER: Power Stretch. Das neue Muskeltraining. BLV Verlagsgesellschaft, München/Wien/Zürich 1993 (2)

GROSSER, M., A. NEUMAIER: Techniktraining. BLV Sportwissen. BLV Verlagsgesellschaft, München/Wien/Zürich 1982

GROSSER, M., S. STARISCHKA, E. ZIMMERMANN, F. ZINTL: Konditionstraining. BLV Sportwissen. BLV Verlagsgesellschaft,

HOLLMANN, W., T. HETTINGER: Sportmedizin. Schattauer, Stuttgart/New York 1990 (3)

LOEHR, J. E.: Die neue mentale Stärke. BLV Verlagsgesellschaft, München/Wien/Zürich 1996

MARÉES, H. DE: Sportphysiologie. Medizin von heute. Tropon Werke 1992 (7)

MARTIN, D.: Training im Kindes- und Jugendalter. Studienbrief 23 der Trainerakademie Köln des Deutschen Sportbundes. Verlag Karl Hofmann, Schorndorf 1988

MEINEL, K., G. SCHNABL: Bewegungslehre – Sportmotorik. Verlag Volk und Wissen, Berlin 1988 (8)

MUNTER, W.: Merkblatt zur Beurteilung der Lawinengefahr. ESSM, Magglingen 1994

NEDIM, C. H.: Technikanalyse und Techniktraining. Academia Verlag, Sankt Augustin 1991

PLATZER, W.: Taschenatlas der Anatomie. Band 1: Bewegungsapparat. Georg Thieme Verlag, Stuttgart/New York 1986 (5)

SCHNABL, G.: Trainingswissenschaft. Sportverlag, Berlin 1994

SIEBERT, W.: Lawinenkunde für Anfänger, Fortgeschrittene und Experten. Österreichischer Bundesverlag, Wien 1984

SILBERNAGL, S., A. DESPOPOULOS: Taschenatlas der Physiologie. Georg Thieme Verlag, Stuttgart/New York 1991 (4)

SLEAMAKER, R.: Systematisches Leistungstraining. Meyer & Meyer Verlag, Aachen 1991

SWIX: SWIX Sport Wachsfibel, 1996

TOKO: Wax Book

WEINECK, J.: Optimales Training. Perimed-Spitta Medizinische Verlagsgesellschaft, Balingen 1994 (8)

WILLIMCZIK, K. (Hg.): Biomechanik der Sportarten. Rowohlt Taschenbuch Verlag, Reinbek 1989

WILLIMCZIK, K., K. ROTH: Bewegungslehre. Rowohlt Taschenbuch Verlag, Reinbek 1991

ZINTL, F.: Ausdauertraining. BLV Sportwissen. BLV Verlagsgesellschaft, München/Wien/Zürich 1994 (3)

Glossary

action time, motor:
speed of movements determined by degree of external resistance

aerobic:
exchange processes in organisms (e.g., musculature) involving oxygen

analyzers:
complexes within the sensory system, consisting of specific receptors and afferent nerve routes (to sensory centers); every analyzer carries parts of information by a sequence of movements

antagonists:
opposing muscles that work together in bending and straightening; antagonists work against the acting agonists and restrict the movement

anthropometric traits:
traits of size and proportion in the human body and its parts

anticipation (also motor anticipation, and movement anticipation):
conscious anticipation of an action (program anticipation) and a result (result anticipation)

center of gravity (body's):
body's mathematically conceived midpoint of mass; the center of gravity is not fixed at any point in the body; its location depends on overall spatial orientation of body

central fatigue:
fatigue of nervous system

centripetal force:
force directed to the axis of spin with complete nonlinear movements, which forces the body in motion into the curve around the axis of rotation when there is a connection between the body and the axis

cognitive arena:
thought processes

concentric muscle contraction:
type of muscle contraction where the muscle fiber length changes; main form of muscle use

contraction speed:
speed with which a muscle or a muscle fiber shortens

coping:
top edge of the halfpipe

curve course:
description of a track in the shape of an arc; the curve course is a function of how the course is set

differentiation, motor:
capacity for optimal coordination of individual movements with regard to parameters of force, time, and space

dynamic muscle work:
organization of muscle work according to physical points of strength development in static (isometric), dynamic-positive (concentric), and dynamic-negative (eccentric) muscle work

eccentric muscle work:
negative dynamic (dropping) muscle work

endogenous factors:
athletic development of certain inner hereditary factors

exogenous factors:
athletic development of external factors

flat:
level part of halfpipe

functional-anatomic viewpoint:
observation of physique or individual body parts with a view toward specific movements and sports

hereditary factors:
ones transmitted through available genetic material

hit:
jump performed on a snowboard

hypertrophy method:
strength-training method for increasing muscle cross-section

hypertrophy (muscular):
thickening of muscle cells that produces greater cross-section and increased muscular strength

ideomotor activity:
muscle movements that are triggered spontaneously by mental imaging

IC method:
strength training method for improving intramuscular coordination and synchronous activation of a large number of muscle fibers in a muscle

imbalance training:
preventive training to eliminate discipline-specific one-sided muscle development

instrumental behavior:
in psychology, direct behavior to alter psychological person-environment-change relationship, e.g., by completing a competition or a performance test in training

intermuscular coordination:
working together of synergistic and antagonistic active muscles in performance of a deliberate move

intramuscular coordination:
coordination of muscle fibers by the central nervous system within a muscle

linking, motor:
ability to join body movements for optimal timing

maximum strength:
strength achieved with maximum intentional contraction against a fixed resistance

move:
action characterized by motor process, whose goal can be achieved only through movements

movement structure:
legitimate, simultaneous, and sequential execution of all elements of a complex movement as a unified whole in time and space

muscle contraction:
shortening of a muscle as a result of an impulse

neurophysiological limitations:
existing limitations between nervous system and the rest of the organism

performance management:
goal-oriented, scientifically supported regulation of training process to maximize performance

periodic training:
phased training for optimal athletic performance

preinnervation:
early twitching of muscle fiber as a result of a nerve impulse for real muscle contraction

psychoregulative training methods:
training methods for creating or maintaining optimal psycho-vegetative conditions as requirement for athletic activity, using influences from self and others

reaction force:
force required to produce highly concentric strength impulse in the shortest time from a braking (eccentric) movement

recruiting:
use of individual muscle fibers for a muscle contraction

reflex innervation:
effect of a nerve impulse that leads to a spontaneous muscle contraction

rehabilitation time:
time necessary for restoration of athletic performance after injuries or illnesses

static muscle work:
external force and tension of muscle are in equilibrium; with static muscle work there is a development of tension, but not a contraction involving any distance (holding work)

synergists:
muscles that perform the same work

torque:
product of force and the distance of its application point from the turning axis

training principles:
ground rules in athletic training with universal applicability

transition:
section between wall and flat inside halfpipe

turning impulse:
impulse of a rotating body as a function of torque and speed of body moving around an axis of rotation

vert:
perpendicular part of wall

Index